THE TIMES OF INDIA

THE SPEAKING TREE

Celebrating Happiness

A Times Group Presentation in Association with

THE SPEAKING TREE - Celebrating Happiness

Copyright ©Bennett, Coleman & Co. Ltd, 2011

Published in 2011

First reprint in 2013

by
Bennett, Coleman & Co. Ltd.
7, Bahadur Shah Zafar Marg
New Delhi-110002

All rights reserved
No part of this work may be reproduced or used in any form or by any means (graphic, electronic, mechanical, photocopying, recording, taping, web distribution, information storage and retrieval systems or otherwise) without prior written permission of the publisher.

Acknowledgements
We thank all those who have contributed to 'The Speaking Tree' column in *The Times of India* over the years.

Edit, Design, Marketed and Distributed by

Times Group Books
(A division of Bennett, Coleman and Company Limited)
Times Annexe, 9-10, Bahadur Shah Zafar Marg, New Delhi-110002

ISBN 978-93-80942-71-1

Printed by
International Print-o-Pac Ltd.

Price: ₹250

PREFACE

For a mainstream newspaper which reports events from around the world, minus a great amount of tampering or analysis, *The Times of India* has been responsible in its mission. For more than a century and a half now, the daily has covered glorious highs as well as pitiful lows. Yet, for a long time there was no sense of a deep-seated satisfaction that came from a job well done.

It was this sense of dissatisfaction, disenchantment and a drive to move beyond mere reporting (mostly of brutalities, death and destruction) that gave rise to The Speaking Tree. This column has been a forum for readers to decipher, understand and accept disturbing events/news in a philosophical way. At a very basic level, it helps readers to cope in an all-too-familiar context the relevance of religion, spirituality and philosophy. At a higher and far more sublime level, these columns assist readers to sift the transient from the permanent, the truth from the web of deception and wisdom from a maze of unfurling lies. It aspires to provide hope and comfort to fatigued minds, turbulent hearts and burdened spirits, and provides security in the knowledge that ultimately it is this hope and the strength derived from it that keeps the human spirit afloat.

The present volume consists of the more stimulating presentations of the column. Every contribution, needless to say, is potent enough to transform human abilities, capabilities and his interface with life and its ebbs. We offer this book to you with the great hope that it will open up your mind and soul, inspire your spirits and become a sweet companion along the walk of your life.

Indu Jain
New Delhi, October 2011

Contents

Introduction 11

What you Might Henceforth Learn at Business School 13
Prakash Shesh

Art of Wise Living Brings Great Joy 15
Swami Sukhabodhananda

Renunciation Keeps Man, Nature Happy 17
Amrit Gangar

Mantra for Happiness: Loving Detachment 19
Amitava Basu

Learn to be Free, to be Joyous 21
Manish Maladkar

Spread Happiness to Connect Effectively 23
Sadhguru Jaggi Vasudev

Spread Happiness in the New Year 25
Osho

Transform your Mind to be Content & Happy 27
Ramesh S Balsekar

The Happiness Factor in Natural Evolution 29
Anil K Rajvanshi

Why Children Smile a Lot & Adults are Grouchy 31
HS Gopalan

Creation Gives you Freedom to Suffer or be Happy 33
Sadhguru Jaggi Vasudev

You Just Need an Excuse to be Joyous .35
Sadhguru Jaggi Vasudev

Happiness is not Simply a Passing State of Mind 37
Ananda Wood

The Spiritual Light Cast by Laughter 39
Marguerite Theophil

Pathways to Peace & Happiness 41
Mata Amritanandamayi

Joy or Misery, you Choose 43
Dinesh Kumar

Success & Joy: The Difference 45
Geet Sethi

Life is Celebration, be Happy 47
Shashin

Attain Peace & Joy: Change yourself 49
Sadhguru Jaggi Vasudev

Stress-free Action Brings Peace & Joy 51
Alok Chopra

Celebrating Bliss which is Brahman 53
Pravin Shanker Mehta

Bliss as the State beyond Happiness 55
Vijay T Salve

Community Welfare & Individual Happiness 57
Bharat Dogra

The Gateway to Bliss 59
Jaya Row

Lakshmi's Lotus of Perfect Happiness 61
KM Gupta

Happiness through Head & Heart 63
Dada JP Vaswani

Feeling Blissful is only the Beginning 65
Sadhguru

Think Positive to be Pain-free & Happy 67
Mahi Pal

Yogic Steps to Achieve Success & Happiness 69
Swami Kriyananda

Find the Right Track to Achieve Bliss 71
Sonam Tsomo

Let's overcome Stress as Children of Bliss 73
Swami Vishvas

Happiness doesn't Happen to Us, it Happens by Us 75
Marguerite Theophil

Guru Retails Bliss, not Happiness 77
Vithal C Nadkarni

Affluence cannot Bring Lasting Happiness 79
Satyendra Garg

The Parable of the Blissful Madman 81
Jahanavi Shandilya

Gross National Happiness Indicates True State 83
Amitava Basu

Enjoy to the Hilt the Joy of Being 85
Swami Kriyananda

When Bliss Alone Exists, can there be Sorrow? 87
Swami Chidananda

Decipher the Formula of Happiness 89
Kiran Bedi

Look for Happiness in the Right Places 91
B Vichar Vishnu Maharaj

Mathematical Equation for Eternal Happiness 93
KS Iyer

Learn where to Look for Happiness 95
Swami Sukhabodhananda

Vedantic Life of Action, Peace & Happiness 97
Swamy Parthasarathy

The Way to Achieve Lasting Happiness 99
Swami Tejomayananda

Joy is your Very Nature, Make it Sustainable 101
Sadhguru

Joy is Short-lived, Bliss is Eternal 103
Ashutoshji Maharaj

Happiness is Temporary, Bliss is Eternal 105
Swami Kriyananda

Give up Pleasure so you can Know Bliss 107
B Ballabh Tirtha Maharaj

All Art is Spiritual, Blissful Experience 109
ML Varadpande

Be both Blissful & Socially Compatible 111
Sadhguru

Keep it Simple & you'll be Happy 113
Dada J P Vaswani

Feeling Blissful is Only the Beginning 115
Sadhguru

Many Paths to Bliss 117
Shri Nimishananda

A Bliss beyond Words 119
Vivek Jain

Finding Purpose in the Flow 122
Nergis Dalal

Love 24X7 Takes you to the State of Everlasting Joy 124
Thich Nhat Hanh

Knowledge, Not Experience, is Path to Anubhava 126
Swami Dayananda

Logical Deduction for Happiness in Life 128
Ramesh Balsekar

For Happy Living Follow Two Rules 130
L Ron Hubbard

Less Possessions, More Happiness 132
Anil K Rajvanshi

I am not Suffering, I am Happiness 134
Vinay Kamat

Happiness Lies in Mind Control 136
Shri Aasaramji Bapu

Follow Dharma to Attain Bliss 138
Shri Maheswar Pathak

Lasting Happiness Comes from within 140
Harsh Kabra

Discover the secret of Happiness within 142
Deepak Nigam

No more Questions, only Bliss 144
RK Gupta

Self-awareness can Bring Happiness 146
Swami Bodhananda

Siddha Maha Yoga can Bring about Positive Changes 148
AM Kulkarni

Happiness is not Everything 150
Swami Brahmdev

Contentment is the Kernel of Happiness 152
Sukhvinder Singh

It's Absolute Bliss, within & without 154
Purushottam Mahajan

Friendliness Brings Happiness & Health 156
Acharya Mahaprajna

Surrender the Ego, Attain Happiness 159
Ullhas Pagey

Young & Dejected? Here's some Cheer 161
MPK Kutty

Para Vidya, Path to Eternal Bliss 163
Shri Ashutoshji Maharaj

Ultimate Pledge for Lasting Happiness 165
Shri Aasaramji Bapu

Thinking it through, you can be Happy 167
Anil K Rajvanshi

The Small Boy & the Leaf 169
  Vinay Kamat

Give it all Up for the Sake of Bliss 171
  Osho

The Ultimate Joy is Inner Growth 173
  Swami Sukhabodhananda

Why Small Things can Shatter Happiness 175
  RD Parkar

In Search of Happiness 177
  Anup Taneja

Peace Feeds Happiness 179
  Oswald Pereira

Scriptural Psychotherapy & Happiness 181
  Hasmukh Adhia

The Joyful Child is the Father of Man 183
  Radhika Nagarth

Introduction

am still determined to be cheerful and happy, in whatever situation I may be; for I have also learned from experience that the greater part of our happiness or misery depends upon our dispositions, and not upon our circumstances —
Martha Washington.

These are the words of the wife of George Washington, the first president of the United States of America. And time and again her sentiments reflect the age-old truth that happiness has less to do with circumstance than with our attitude and approach to life. Each of us is the creator of our own thoughts and state of mind. This does not mean ignoring the often, painful reality of what happens, but understanding that you can choose your response to something at any given moment. This volume of The Speaking Tree culls articles from *The Times of India* that have appeared over the years in the column by the same name. The theme for this volume is 'happiness'.

What is happiness? In simple words, it is a feeling which imparts pleasure in us, which could be derived by fulfilling a long-cherished dream or meeting a dear one or walking by the sea. Happiness has different shades of meaning depending upon the way we perceive it. According to Osho a happy person is not one who is always happy but one who is happy even in unhappiness.

Krishna relates in the *Bhagavad Gita* that all living beings are made up of soul, gross body and subtle body. Soul is the master of the body and is composed of *sat-chit-ananda* or everlasting happiness. Though we are made up of happiness, still we look for happiness in external objects. Happiness is a state of mind. So why are we looking for happiness outside? That is because we lack knowledge about ourselves. We study to become successful so that we become happy. Not all of us know where to seek happiness. We run after money, power, wealth, authority, status, name and fame. But in reality we are running after the shadow of happiness. True happiness comes from within, from a purified mind and a loving heart.

Among those whose articles are featured in the present volume are Osho, Swami Sukhabodhananda, Marguerite Theophil and Swami Kriyananda. All of them have their own take on happiness. However, a common thread running through their thoughts is that happiness is the true nature of every human being and that we all should learn to be happy from within to be able

Introduction

What you Might Henceforth Learn at Business School

Prakash Shesh

Good business schools are becoming aware that apart from learning how to maximize wealth, they need to also learn how to maximize happiness — their own and of those around them. There is a difference between happiness and what we describe as joy and pleasure. On a warm day what a glass of cold lemon juice gives you is pleasure for it is momentary and sensory. Happiness, on the other hand, is experienced in the mind and is therefore infinitely more powerful.

Are we happier today than we were a hundred years ago? If we're not, isn't it amazing that technological aids have not been able to add to our happiness? What could we do to feel happy or happier?

1. Identify what makes you happy: I have met very few people who are clear about what makes them happy. Since they are unclear about their objectives, they live a perennially unhappy life. List down what will make you happy. Generate goals that are specific, achievable but challenging.

2. Compete with yourself: A study conducted at Harvard demonstrated that people are happier when they are relatively more prosperous than their compatriots. Respondents chose between two situations: a) Your annual salary is $1,00,000 while your compatriot gets $75,000; b) Your annual salary is $1,50,000 while your compatriot gets $1,75,000. Though the salary was more in the (b) situation, respondents overwhelmingly preferred (a). Why not compete with oneself instead of grieving over others' achievements?

3. Don't expect everyone to agree with you: We usually equate disagreement with enmity in spite of knowing that intelligent people rarely agree on anything; every individual has a perspective that's unique. So try and persuade the other person but don't be unhappy if you fail.

4. Live life according to your beliefs: Intellectual independence must follow financial independence. Implement your beliefs without inconveniencing others and be happy.

5. Live in the present: The past is dead and gone. Peep into it only to learn from mistakes. Dream of the future but remember you can't enjoy it until it becomes your present. So don't postpone what you can do today.

6. Increase the sources of your happiness: Gardening, singing, playing an instrument, exercising, meditating...The more the merrier.

7. Limit your desires: We get caught in that vicious spiral of infinite wants. The happiness you derive from moving from one product to another — bigger, better, more expensive — is at best short-lived. Try to figure out what you can do without. Incremental benefits as you climb up the value chain of materialism are fewer than the incremental costs that you might incur.

8. Forgive and forget: Forgiving your opponents who played dirty may not make you a winner but it would surely make you happier. Jealousy and prolonged anger are agents of death.

9. Keep your curiosity alive: People who vigorously retain the childlike habit of questioning are happy on two counts. They enjoy getting to know the answers and their curiosity keeps their mind alive and kicking.

10. Shun hypocrisy: We worship women as goddesses but don't respect them at home, workplace or any other situation. We keep our courtyards clean by dumping garbage in the neighbour's compound or on the street. Double standards don't contribute to happiness.

11. Spend time with the young: Their happiness is infectious and costs nothing.

12. Give liberally: Share your smile, advice, cheer, money, help or just company. Giving should reduce your assets but giving happiness actually increases your own inventory — just try it out!

Art of Wise Living Brings Great Joy

Swami Sukhabodhananda

The art of wise living involves four steps: Plan purposefully, prepare prayerfully, proceed positively and pursue persistently. The joy of wise living involves the art of joyous looking. There are two types of looking. You can look at the world with thoughts; you can also look at the world without thoughts, from a pure Being. When you look at the world with thoughts, then you should be aware of the subtle pollution that exists.

Thoughts come from memory, memory is the representation of an experience of the past, and so from the past you see the present. Hence, pollution happens. Is it not natural that we look at the world through these thoughts? If the answer is 'yes', then the possibility of a higher perception does not exist. You can say, ordinarily, you look through thoughts. However, there is an extraordinary way of looking at life. Have you not observed many physically challenged people doing extraordinary things in life? You might have observed that mental setbacks are harder to cope with than the physical, because it makes people ineffective. They operate from the 'I can't' rather than 'I can'. They operate from scarcity rather than abundance. They are rooted in poverty consciousness rather than in prosperity consciousness. We have to learn the art of coming from abundance rather than from scarcity.

Creativity happens in this space. What does being effective mean? Effective people learn to reduce stress, increase happiness and increase potential. How to reduce stress? There is external and internal stress. External stress involves your eating habits, pollution and erratic sleeping habits. Internal stress involves attitudes, beliefs, dogmas and negative patterns. One has to learn the art of handling them from a spiritual perspective. Meditation is a great way of making this happen. What do people really want in life? Most of us are like a ship in the ocean without a compass. What we want is success and satisfaction. Success is getting what you like and satisfaction is liking what you get.

Reflect on the following exchange between a traveller and a tourist guide. Traveller: "What will be the weather at this point?"

Guide: "The weather is going to be the weather that I like."

Traveller: "How can you get a weather you like?"

Guide: "I don't always get the weather I like. Therefore, I learn to like what I get. So I get a weather that I like."

The art of getting what I like and liking what I get — this, one should cultivate through spiritual practice. The next important point we need to observe is that most of us are searching for happiness. We search for happiness in the world of objects and things. However, we fail to appreciate that the world of objects can give us pleasure but not happiness. People don't see this distinction; hence they suffer in life.

Happiness really exists within. The art of going within is one of the arts we have to learn. Once we discover the art of being happy within, then we will participate in the miracle called life. Have you seen the beauty of the sunrise? Very few people experience the ecstasy of the sunrise. We live in a beautiful world, but we still continue to live in small ponds of misery.

Even when we are pulled out of the ponds of misery, we continue to be in our own misery, for each one is identified with his or her own misery. Once we learn the art of disassociating ourselves from the idea of misery, we will see so much of joy around us. We will participate in the sun rising, the sun setting, we will participate in the twinkling of stars and the moving clouds. The whole world will become a source of joy.

Renunciation Keeps Man, Nature Happy

Amrit Gangar

On September 22, 1931, two icons of the West and the East met in a humble tenement in London. Mahatma Gandhi impressed Charlie Chaplin with his view that supreme independence meant shedding oneself of unnecessary things. Chaplin believed this principle was the basis of Gandhi's political-economic-spiritual argument against machinery. However, what Gandhi told Chaplin that day echoes the Jaina principle of *aparigraha* (the first letter 'a' pronounced as 'u' in upper). Simply put, *aparigraha* means non-possession or non-acquisition. As is well-known, Gandhi was deeply influenced by Jainism.

Right knowledge, right faith and right conduct are the three basic prerequisites for attaining liberation. In order to acquire these qualities, Jainism prescribes observation of the five great vows — *ahimsa* or non-violence; *satya* or truth; *asteya* or non-stealing; *brahmacharya* or celibacy; and *aparigraha* or non-attachment. Acquisition of material goods leads one to attachment and hence pain if, for some reason, the goods or wealth are lost. Happiness is about freedom from pain and hence can only accrue from leading a life of simplicity and non-attachment. That is the message of *aparigraha*. The thrust of *aparigraha* is to create a balanced society with balanced individuals. The absolutely secular principle of *aparigraha* — not to allow greed to dominate our thoughts and actions — can help overcome our tendency to overaccumulate.

Gandhi was right when he said the earth had enough to satisfy the needs of all the people, but not for satisfying the greed of some. Here lies the subtle difference between 'need' and 'want'. Jainism believes that the more worldly wealth a person possesses, the more likely is he to commit sin to acquire the possession, and in the process be unhappy. Worldly wealth creates attachments, which will continually give rise to greed, jealousy, selfishness, ego, hatred and violence. Attachments to worldly objects result in bondage to the cycle of birth and death. Therefore, one who desires of spiritual liberation should withdraw from all attachments to objects of all the five senses.

Practical wisdom tells us that anything in excess is harmful. Overconsumption or overacquisition affects our social environment just as environmental degradation affects our physical survival. *Aparigraha* can be interpreted in multi-faceted ways — preserving nature, conserving energy and living austerely. The kind of inequity that prevails in the world today is alarming. Statistics inform us that over the last four years the world's 200 richest people have doubled their wealth to more than $1tn, while 1.3bn people are living on less than a dollar a day. The affliction of consumerism promises to get worse as the system insists on finding new ways to exploit people and the environment.

If everyone practises *aparigraha*, how pure and peaceful our world would be! In the contemporary context of globalization, the applied theory of *aparigraha* can work as a good interventionist and ecological measure to retain the balance between man and nature. Far-sighted Gandhi realized its value — both in strategic and spiritual terms. Every action of his suggested that he was a practising environmentalist, long before environmental protection became fashionable in the West and elsewhere. In the modern world, Gandhi provided us an alternative model of development we forgot to remember. In a nutshell, renunciation through *aparigraha* could end in more genuine peace and happiness for all.

Mantra for Happiness: Loving Detachment

Amitava Basu

Simply put, happiness is satisfaction of mind. However, different individuals have different perceptions of how to achieve happiness. For some, happiness lies in wealth; for others, it is in rank and position; yet others find happiness in fame and name. Commonly, happiness is measured by achievement in terms of money, property, other material possessions, power, name, fame, education, lifestyle, position and social status. In their quest for happiness individuals tread a path that destroys the inner good instincts and virtues. Craving for material wealth begets greed and greed leads to corruption. Similar is the outcome when passion for power drives one's mind.

Life is not permanent; nothing in life can last forever. Saints and sages have realized this truth and lived away from pursuit of mundane objects and worldliness. But ordinary people fail to see this truth. Maya impels individuals to believe that material achievement is the truth of life; and, in the process, it fuels attachment to worldly pursuits and sensory pleasures. Growing attachment breeds addiction to material attainments. In turn, such addiction intoxicates the human mind, making it oblivious to the truth. So real happiness remains a mirage.

Mahasiddha Naropa, the tenth century *mahasiddha* of the Kagya School of Tibetan Buddhism, was born in a rich and powerful family. He renounced his family and wealth at the age of 25 to be ordained as a monk-scholar in Nalanda University where he became a leading scholar and respected faculty member. He later left in search of a guru to attain *moksha* and found Tilopa, who was one of the four *mahasiddhas* of India. Once Tilopa handed a string full of knots to Naropa and asked him to untie them. Naropa did so and gave the string back to Tilopa. Tilopa threw the string away and asked Naropa what he understood. Naropa replied that all beings are tied by worldly attachments and they need to untie themselves.

Dispassion for attachment to material pleasures and comforts restrains one's desires, dispels worries and fears and guides us to the path of peace and tranquillity. To be dispassionate, you need to search your heart everyday and practise untying your passion for mundane matters. An individual who meticulously endeavours to get rid of expectations, hopes and fears can set the mind at rest and reach a stage of detachment from worldly pleasures. This, however, cannot be achieved overnight. This change needs preparation of the mind and takes time. It is a practice that an individual needs to pursue for 'being in the world but not of it'. You should have a mind open to everything but attached to nothing. This does not mean that you have to run away from your family, society, duties and responsibilities and be less sensitive. One needs to recognize the Divine in others and work to serve the Divine.

Some may argue that the incentive behind every work is gain, without which an individual will not be motivated to work. Then how will the detachment happen? The gain is realization of what is Eternal and the alleviation of material suffering following from this realization.

Sri Guru Granth Sahib says, "As the lotus flower floats unaffected in the water, so should one remain detached in one's own household." The lotus flower is not tainted by the slime in which it grows. It is an attitude that an individual needs to develop through belief and practice; and only this can emancipate one from worldly attachments to derive pure happiness.

Learn to be Free, to be Joyous

Manish Maladkar

Each day is a chance to invest in life; a chance to renew yourself. To shed yesterday's skin. To unburden yourself. To get rid of yesterday's hurt. Be glad of life each day as it gives you a chance to work, love and play to look at the sun. And then when the sun sets, don't cry — the tears will make you miss the beauty of the stars.

Life moves on and if you don't stop and look at the wonders already present in your life, you will miss life altogether. Think of big thoughts but relish the small joys life offers you each day. Maybe it's as simple as smiling at someone. For that could be the last day of life — for you or for her. A small genuine act from you will cost you nothing but it could mean everything to somebody that day. Life is a succession of moments. Live each moment. Life has no romance without risk. Any action carries some amount of risk, may be less or more, but the element of risk is always present. If there is no wind row. Make things happen rather than let things happen. One can give nothing whatsoever without giving oneself, risking oneself. The most important thing in life is not what you get but what you give.

Once a preacher called at the home of a very poor family. When he came out he found one son admiring his new car, so the preacher explained that he had received it as a gift from his brother. Most lads would say, "Wish I had a brother like that." But this one said, "Mister, I wish I could be a brother like that."

If you are not enjoying this journey, for sure you won't enjoy the destination. It will become a moment to dread, not a moment you can actually look forward to. It's not what happens that determines our future, but what you do about what happens that counts. Make the most of life. Earn all that you can, save all that you can, and give all that you can. Although greed comes from the desire to obtain something, it is not satisfied by obtaining. The true antidote of greed is contentment. Take yourself less seriously. Conquer the mind and you conquer the world. Looking back strains your neck muscles. Similarly, living in the past strains your life. Don't dwell on the past, have faith in yourself and you will have faith in others. Fulfil your destiny. Remember, no one can make you unhappy without your consent. The way you cope with life, is what makes the difference. Even peace of mind is not the absence of conflict but the ability to cope with it. You have to reach out to other people. That will teach you to forgive people and also forgive yourself. Forgiveness means letting go of the past, having compassion about stepping outside yourself. A kind compassionate act is often it's own reward. Live your life without complaining, just like the tree.

We cannot stop suffering in the world. But we can stop it in our mind, provided you know your mind, which is the source of negative thoughts. Only you can doctor your mind. Your happiness is dependent on consistency. When you experience inconsistency you experience disappointments, resentments and self-pity, guilt and grief. Learn to be free, learn to be joyous. Learn to let go if someone passes away. Learn to forgive yourself and others. Once you are free the fear of death will trouble you no longer.

Spread Happiness to Connect Effectively

Sadhguru Jaggi Vasudev

You deal with people and situations effectively only when you are happy. Otherwise, in your unhappiness, it won't matter what good intentions you have, you will only spread misery in the world. Being happy or unhappy is actually your choice. People have chosen to be unhappy because they think that by being unhappy they will get something. Once you are unhappy, whatever you get, what does it matter? If you are happy, if you don't get anything, what does it matter? This is not a philosophy; this is your true nature. By nature you want to be happy. Every creature wants to be happy. Everything that you are doing, every single act you are performing is in pursuit of happiness in some way. Why would you want to serve people? Serving people gives you happiness; that is why you serve them. Somebody wants to wear good clothes; somebody wants to make a lot of money, because that gives them happiness.

Whatever every human being is doing on this planet, it does not matter what, even if he is giving away his life to somebody, he is doing it because it gives him happiness. So happiness is the fundamental goal of life. Why do you want to go to heaven? Only because you've been told that if you go to heaven, you will be happy.

After doing all that you are doing, if happiness is not happening, somewhere you have missed the ABCs of life, the fundamentals. When you were a child, you were simply happy. Without doing anything, you were happy. Then somewhere along the way, you lost this. Why did you lose it? You got deeply identified with many things around you, your body, your mind. What you call your mind is actually just the stuff you have picked up from social situations around you. The kind of mind you have depends on the kind of society you have been exposed to. Everything in your mind right now is something you picked up from outside. You got so identified with it, now it is causing you misery.

This body is not yours; you have picked it up from the earth. You were born with a tiny body, which your parents gave you. After that, you ate plants and animals and grew. You borrowed it from the earth; it is not yours. For a while you have to use it, so enjoy it and go. But you have become so deeply identified with it, you think this is you. No wonder you suffer. The basis of all this misery is, you have established yourself in untruth. You are deeply identified with that which you are not. Hence the suffering.

The whole process of spirituality is only to de-identify with that which you are not. When you don't know what you really are, can you search for it? If you search, only your imagination will run wild. If you start thinking, "Who am I?" somebody will tell you that you are God's child. Somebody else will tell you that you are the devil's child. Somebody might tell you something else, endless beliefs... So, the only thing that you can do is, whatever you are not, start discounting that. When everything is discounted there is something, which cannot be discounted. When you arrive at that, you will see, there is no reason for misery in this world.

Spread Happiness in the New Year

Osho

Laughter is the best medicine. If you can laugh when you are ill you will get your health back sooner. If you cannot laugh, even if you are healthy, sooner or later you will lose your health and you will become ill. Laughter brings inner energy to the fore. When you really laugh, for those few moments you are in a deep meditative state. Thinking stops. It is impossible to laugh and think together. When you really laugh, suddenly, the mind disappears. And the whole Zen methodology is how to get into no-mind.

Dancing and laughter are the best, natural, easily approachable doors to attaining no-mind. Existence melts into you; there is an overlapping of boundaries. And if you are really dancing — not managing it but allowing it to manage you, allowing it to possess you — if you are possessed by dance, thinking stops. The same happens with laughter. If you are possessed by laughter, thinking stops. And if you know a few moments of no-mind, those glimpses will promise you many more rewards that are going to come.

Before the mind disappears there open two alternatives: sleep or *sushupti/ samadhi* and *satori*. When thinking disappears, these are the two alternatives left: either you move into satori — a fully alert, no-thought state; or a fully asleep, no-thought state — sleep. And sleep is more natural, because you have practised it long. If you live 60 years, for 20 years you have been asleep. It is the greatest activity that you have been doing; one-third of your life is spent in sleep. Laughing, how can you fall asleep? It brings a state of no-mind and no-thought, and does not allow you to fall asleep.

In a few Zen monasteries, every monk has to start his morning with laughter, and has to end his night with laughter. It will be difficult, living in a family set-up, to suddenly laugh early in the morning. But do try it; it's worth getting out of bed laughing. Yes, for no reason at all. Isn't it good to be alive? One day you will not get up in the morning. One day the milkman will knock at the door, the spouse will be snoring, but you will not be there. One day, death will come. Before it knocks you down, have a good laugh — while there is time, have a good laugh.

And look at the whole ridiculousness: again the same day starts; you have done the same things again and again for your whole life. Again you will get into your slippers, rush to the bathroom — for what? Brushing your teeth, taking a shower — for what? Where are you going? Getting ready and nowhere to go!

Look at the whole ridiculousness of it — and have a good laugh. Laughter leads to more laughter. And almost always I have seen people doing just the wrong thing. From early morning they get out of bed complaining, gloomy, sad, depressed, and miserable. Then one thing leads to another — and for nothing. And they get angry... it is very bad because it will change your climate for the whole day, it will set a pattern for the whole day.

In their insanity, Zen people are saner than you are. They start the day laughing. Then the whole day you will feel laughter bubbling, welling up. There are so many ridiculous things happening all over! God must be dying of laughter — down the centuries, for eternity, seeing this ridiculousness of the world. The people that He has created, and all the absurdities — it is really a comedy. He must be laughing. If you become silent after your laughter, one day you will hear God also laughing, you will hear the whole existence laughing with you — even the trees and stones and stars.

Transform your Mind to be Content & Happy

Ramesh S Balsekar

It is precisely the pursuit of happiness which prevents happiness from happening and, until this realization happens, the pursuit must go on. What is seeking happiness is consciousness. Impersonal consciousness had identified itself with a particular body-minded organism (form) and a name as a separate entity; and it is this trapped, unidentified consciousness which is seeking its personality. When the ego, the practical seeker of everything in life, takes over the search for happiness, pleasure is mistaken for happiness in the flow of life... The few egos that focus on real happiness become spiritual seekers, for they realize that what they are seeking is not to be found in the flow of life, but in their attitude.

The Greek word metanoesis implies changing the mind, but means transformation of mind. The Sanskrit word for it is *paravritti*, meaning turning around at the deepest level of the heart-mind. *Paravritti* tells the seeker-ego that happiness is one's natural state, hidden by hatred born of our perception of the 'other' as a source of potential rivalry and enmity. We're instructed from childhood that life means competition with the other, and happiness means success over the other, in the classroom as well as playing fields. The other is seen as a potential enemy.

Whether or not we achieve happiness is based on our sense of personal doership. Buddha said, "Events happen, deeds get done, consequences happen, but there is no individual doer of any deed. Everything in life is happening according to Cosmic Law." What the sense of personal doership has done is that the human being, at any moment, is burdened with an enormous load of hatred for oneself for harming others, willingly or otherwise, and also for the others who hurt us. The total acceptance of personal non-doership means the immediate removal of this load of hatred, and the absence of hatred automatically means the presence of our natural state: happiness, consisting of total peace and harmony.

The Sanskrit term *sat-chit-ananda* means Existence-Consciousness-*Ananda*. *Ananda* is *shanti* or peace, not joy or ecstasy. The Buddha said that enlightenment means the end of suffering. It is interesting that the Buddha has used the negative perspective — end of suffering — rather than the positive one of joy or ecstasy. It is the experience of all of us, sometime or the other, that the sudden end of an intense pain has brought about an intensity of relief that was much more acceptable than any positive pleasure or joy. Pursuit of happiness is the very essence of living for all creatures on earth, beginning with the infant seeking its mother's breast. For the poor, happiness can only mean sufficient money to provide the minimum of food, clothing and shelter. But for those who are reasonably comfortable in life, it is the destiny of a few to look for their happiness beyond what the flow of life could bring. In the case of the unselfish and generous, being generous gives them the happiness they seek, and not being generous would make them unhappy.

Ultimately, happiness means not something in the flow of life, it is the attitude to life. And the most important point about it is that there is no 'doing' in it. It is a pure happening.

The Happiness Factor in Natural Evolution

Anil K Rajvanshi

In a riverbed were two trees. One was the mighty Banyan tree and the other was a reed. "You are spineless; look at me. Not only am I tall and stand erect, I also give shade to the weary," it would often say to the reed. In the rainy season came a flash flood that uprooted the banyan tree. The reed, however, survived as it simply bent with the current and when the floods receded it became erect again. This is a story of the strength of humility. Another great lesson the story contains is that it is only those systems that come in equilibrium with the surroundings that survive.

Evolution of natural systems normally takes place via branching when the system goes far from equilibrium or 'becomes unwieldy', and is governed by laws of non-linear thermodynamics. The branch which comes into equilibrium with the surrounding forces survives and prospers. Coming into equilibrium with surroundings also means actively interacting with surrounding forces like sun, wind, atmosphere and gravity. A system can only interact with the surrounding forces when it can sense them. Thus natural systems have developed mechanisms for sensing all these elements and hence have temperature, humidity, solar, chemical and gravity sensors.

Most times we are unhappy because of conflict within the self or with the surroundings. To resolve the conflict or come 'in equilibrium' we should be able to sense our surroundings. The first mechanism for happiness is therefore to become acutely aware of the surroundings and corresponding forces. This means developing a sensitive mind and increasing one's awareness. Both these are produced by making our minds powerful through Yoga. A powerful mind is a great information processor and hence can process signals and information from the surroundings very efficiently. Without awareness the interaction with the forces is only a one way affair, that is, we are controlled by them.

This enhanced awareness also helps us become non-violent towards nature and our fellow human beings because we can start understanding the other person's point of view. Similarly, it also gives us strength to make others aware of our point of view. This is the genesis of coming in equilibrium with the surroundings. If we approach a conflict, which could either be internal or external, in the spirit of compromise, then it has a mechanism to elicit a corresponding sentiment from the other person. This results in conflict resolution. Compromising nevertheless is not an easy process. It requires courage and quality thought to produce compromise formulas since a viable and an acceptable solution has to be provided. Gandhiji had made this compromise process into an art form and it was the reason for his success in finding solutions to difficult problems.

The ability to compromise is the second mechanism of happiness. Without compromise, the evolutionary path will be based on conflicts and may end in all-round destruction of both people and environment. This is the path that is being conflict resolution through mechanisms of awareness and compromise can produce true sustainability and happiness.

Why Children Smile a Lot & Adults are Grouchy

HS Gopalan

appiness is a state of mind. External factors like wealth, money, and the comforts they bring by themselves cannot make you happy. Buddha said all earthly possessions and trappings are bondages which bring miseries. Happiness is a state brought about by your being satisfied with what you have got. Be mentally prepared for whatever befalls you. It is only when you develop a sense of not being satisfied with what you have got and crave for more and more that happiness drifts away and unhappiness sets in.

We smile when something pleasant or pleasurable happens. A smile is an involuntary reflection of happiness. Many simple and small things which cost us nothing make us smile. Meeting a beloved, friend or relative, seeing the sun breaking through the clouds after a dark rainy day, a rainbow, a sudden gentle breeze on a hot afternoon, all these things make us happy and light up our face.

Look at a newborn. Within a few days she starts smiling on seeing a recognisable face. What makes her smile? The child smiles and laughs on seeing a toy, by looking at the moon. It is her reaction to being pleased and satisfied. A child smiles 400 to 500 times a day and when we grow into adults the number of smiles per day comes down drastically. A child does not have much expectation. She is happy because she is pleased with whatever she gets. One could always be like a child — in a state of happiness by being satisfied and contented with one's lot. Though difficult to achieve, it is not impossible.

Happiness can also be achieved by realizing that things could have been worse. But it is not in this negative sense alone that one can be happy. Whenever we are unhappy, we should try to recollect and remember how much happiness has come our way and the number of things we have, for which we should be thankful. We should count our blessings and look at the silver lining in the clouds.

We blame God for whatever we are not blessed with, but do we praise God enough for everything he has blessed us with? Are we making best use of whatever we have got? There are innumerable things in life to be happy about. We are blessed with physical abilities, mental faculties, relatives and friends and with nature's bounties. The rest is what we make. Being contented does not imply that we should not be ambitious, but ambition should be within limits and should not turn into avarice. You can have ambition to earn more money through legitimate means, so that you can not only improve your standard of living but also contribute generously to the community. But while doing so one should not get so attached to material gains and comforts that even their temporary absence makes you feel miserable. The scriptures say we should be like a lotus in a pond which gets wet yet allows no drop of water to get stuck to it.

All religions talk of overcoming selfishness, to become selfless. Real happiness will come when one can get liberated to reach a state of nirvana. Nirvana is a state of perfect happiness, an ideal state where one reaches a transcendent consciousness in which there is neither suffering, desire nor sense of self and the subject is released from the effects of karma.

Creation Gives you Freedom to Suffer or be Happy

Sadhguru Jaggi Vasudev

If Creation is perfect, and the Creator has done such a good job, why is there so much suffering? It is such a perfect job that it gives you the opportunity to be whichever way you wish to be. If Creation had not given you this opportunity, then there would be no possibilities, there would be no such thing as liberation. So why create bondage and then liberation? Why couldn't you have just been liberated? Then there would be no Creation. Only because there is Creation, now there is the possibility of going beyond that.

In other forms of life, there is not much possibility other than to survive, procreate, and die one day. So there is not misery either. Their suffering is purely physical. Even in pain, they do not know the kind of suffering that a human being knows. As a human being, you know this suffering not because Creation gave the suffering to you. Creation just gave you the freedom to make whatever you wish to out of yourself. You're making suffering out of yourself, that is your choice.

Physical realities are sometimes comfortable and sometimes not. We have been given the intelligence to create comfort for ourselves. That's not an issue — if we have no problems with each other, creating comfort for all is not a big problem. But simply because we have inner problems, this freedom which should have been a benediction, has become a curse.

Right now, what human beings are suffering is not their bondage; they are suffering their freedom. If you suffer your bondage, it's all right, but if you suffer your freedom that's a tragedy. You can make joy or suffering out of yourself. If almost 90 per cent of the people choose to make misery out of themselves, what can be done? That's not Creation's fault. Creation just gave you the freedom so that you could go beyond. Most people's intelligence is such, they keep their brain in cold storage, for 'future use'. So they only seek the beyond when something really goes wrong with their life. Until then, even if something goes wrong, they will only pray for a better life next time.

Is life of excess a life of joy? The affluent live a life of excess. But this has to change, because as Mahatma Gandhi said, "There is enough in this world for everybody's need, but there is not enough even for one man's greed." There is no end to what a man would want to do to himself to enhance his own grandeur. But somewhere, every human being should be able to place a limit. Some self-restraint is required. Otherwise, your life becomes one of excess. There is no joy in it; people will become totally frustrated and mentally broken. This is happening to the affluent classes of the world everywhere. Money should have brought well-being, but for most people it is bringing terrible situations within themselves.

Whether we make a safety pin or a big machine, or anything, you dig it out of the planet, and there is a certain limit to it. We don't have to live on goat's milk, but somewhere it has to be capped, otherwise this will just lead to destruction of the planet.

You Just Need an Excuse to be Joyous

Sadhguru Jaggi Vasudev

The whole science and wisdom of what we refer to as inner engineering means not seeing joy as something that we could achieve in our life but seeing joy as the very basis of our lives. Joy is not the only goal; but other wonderful things can happen only if this happens. Otherwise, you'll live constantly with the fear of misery haunting you. At every stage in your life, you thought 'If I get this job, this is it, my life is made', but a few years down the line the same job gave you diabetes and blood pressure. You thought 'If I get married, that's it, my life is made', and you know what happened after that!

Life strikes back because many of you are not in tune with your own basic existence and not because there is something wrong with Creation. You have gotten identified with petty things that you gathered. You have become an accumulation; you have no existence of your own. If there is no foundation of joy, I cannot do what I intend to do with people — it doesn't matter who you are, where you are or what you are. I'm constantly laying the foundation in people that they are always trying to uproot. Laying the foundation is not in terms of teaching, not in terms of understanding. Joy is not because you know something, joy is not because you understand something, joy is because the deepest core of you functions finds expression.

When you sit with me, my energies are such that naturally your physical body, your mind and your emotions get aligned in a certain way, so you feel joyful. It is like how an induction motor works — just the flow of energy in one part induces an energy flow in another part. Although the induction is from outside, the actual joy is always from within. In poetic ways we would say 'I will shower joy upon you'. But no, we cannot shower joy upon you. We can create a situation where you cannot but help being aligned in a certain way whereby you naturally feel joyful.

Joy is always an inner experience. If it was showered upon you, your skin should feel it first, but that's not how it happens. So a certain alignment happens within you that naturally allows your innermost core to find expression and joy. For ages, there were scholars, priests, kings and others, but always, a spiritually realized person was held in highest esteem even above the gods simply because their very presence was an instrument to set everything right.

There's nothing else wrong with people except that they're miserable, isn't it? In whatever they do or don't do, they make themselves miserable. They just need an excuse. You will see if you're in a certain level of alignment on a particular day, suddenly you will find that all you need is an excuse to burst into laughter. But if you're in a certain level of misalignment, all you need is an excuse to burst into tears and depression. So you need to understand that whatever you consider right now as the source of your joy is just an excuse.

Happiness is not Simply a Passing State of Mind

Ananda Wood

We usually think of 'happiness' as a state of mind, which alternates with an opposite state called 'unhappiness'. To be 'unhappy' is to feel at odds with the circumstances in which one finds oneself. To be 'happy' is to feel at one with 'hap', the happenings that take place in one's experience. But does this mean that happiness is just a passing state? Is it just a warm, gooey feeling of sentimental pleasure — which must necessarily give way to the cold, hard facts of pain and hunger and want suffered by our vulnerable and petty personalities, in an often hostile and alien world?

The very word 'happiness' suggests that there is something more to it than this. Quite literally, 'happiness' is that shared principle which is common to all 'hap', to all the happenings that take place in the physical and mental world. In this literal sense, happiness is what Aristotle called 'the unmoved mover'. It is the common principle of motivation that inspires all acts and happenings. It is that for which all acts are done, for which all happenings take place, in everyone's experience and in the entire world.

As it is put in the Taittiriya Upanishad (2 7): "It is just this essential savour that is spontaneous and natural. It's only when one reaches this essential savour that one comes to happiness. For what could be alive at all what could move with energy if there were not this happiness here at the background of all space and time, pervading the entire world?"

How can we reconcile these two views of happiness? How can happiness be, on the one hand, a passing state of sentimental mind, and on the other hand, the continuing ground of all motivation? The answer is that passing states of happiness somehow express an underlying ground of value which does not pass away. When an object is desired, the desiring mind is dissatisfied. It feels insufficient in itself, and seeks some object that is thought to be outside This is the state of 'duality' where experience seems divided into two, by thinking that a knowing person is different from some object that is known. This divided and dissatisfied state is what we call 'unhappiness'.

When a desired object is attained, the desiring mind comes temporarily to rest, so that its division and dissatisfaction are for the moment dissolved. This is a state of 'non-duality': where experience no longer seems divided, because the knower is at one with what is known. Here, where dissatisfied desire has given way to a non-dual state of fulfilment, we experience happiness. In this non-dual state of happiness, there is only undivided consciousness, entirely self-contained, unmixed with any alien object that is known outside. The object that was previously desired has now been attained, and is at one with consciousness.

The previously desiring mind is now at rest and has dissolved in consciousness. What is the source of happiness that shines out in this non-dual state? It cannot be the desired object, for the mind soon gets fed up with this particular object and starts agitating for something else. The moment that the mind thus rises up, the state of happiness has passed; so it cannot be from the risen mind that happiness appears. All happiness must come from underlying consciousness: which continues at the background of experience, while the mind changes from one state of experience to another. In this ground of consciousness, there are no alien objects, nor is there any kind of division. It is pure consciousness — non-dual and undivided, entirely self-contained. It is just this that shines spontaneously, in all our states of happiness. It is just this that seems obscured, in all our minds' unhappiness.

Whether we understand it correctly, or whether we do not, it is the ground of happiness from which all acts and happenings arise: the ground we cannot help but seek. As it is put in the Brihadaranyaka Upanishad (4.3.32): "The fluctuating ocean of the many-seeming world turns out to be one single see-er, beyond duality.... This is one's final state. This is one's final happiness. "All other things that have but come to be subsist upon only a measure of this happiness."

The Spiritual Light Cast by Laughter

Marguerite Theophil

In struggling to come to terms with an understanding of a moral philosophy or a detailed analysis of consciousness, we can sometimes lose sight of the fact that the Teaching is essentially a Way of Life rather than a bundle of dried-out abstractions. We try hard to maintain the correct posture during meditation, for instance; or, if involved in ritual, to observe the correct sequence and tone and gesture. All very necessary too; but we can turn all this into merely serious business, imposing a grim, humourless intentness on the joy of the spiritual experience. This tendency is most pronounced in the understanding of Buddhism: it is very easy to attribute only a heavy solemnity to Buddhism, particularly in its earlier forms. A Zen 'Teaching Story' tells us of four pupils of the Tendai school, who promised one another to observe seven days of silence. On the first day, this silence was carried through, but at night, when the oil lamps started to flicker and grow dim, one of them could not help instructing a servant, "Fix those lamps."

The second turned to him in disapproval, "We are not supposed to say a word."

A third scolded them: "You two are stupid; why did you talk?"

And the fourth smugly declared, "I am the only one who hasn't said a thing."

Humour, and the laughter that arises from it, is far beyond funny stories; it is more a recognition of the basic irony of the juxtaposition of extremes. So that, as Chogyam Trungpa, the Tibetan teacher, has written, "One is not caught taking them seriously, so that one does not seriously play their game of hope and fear." Or again, it means seeing both poles of a situation from a detached perspective; you get to see both 'points of view' and to understand their differences as being simply parts of a greater whole.

There is both gentle humour and deep truth when a teacher answers the question, "How do you see things so clearly?" with: "I close my eyes." We often come across this expression of humour in the seventeen-syllable Japanese verse form, the *haiku*. Apart from a statement of feeling or a brush-stroke picture of nature, the *haiku* often expresses an implied identity between two seemingly different things, or strips away pomposity to reveal a fragile and funny truth.

This, for me, is beautifully illustrated in a poem by Issa, a simple provincial poet who brought to his verses his sincere, light-hearted view of life. The setting to be imagined here is the huge, awesome statue of Lord Buddha, out in the open, some time in winter, and the rustic, personal voice of Issa in a seemingly irreverent yet tenderly witty verse:

Buddha on the hill
From your holy nose indeed
Hangs an icicle.

With laughter, free of malice, constant carefree laughter at everything and everyone, including and especially oneself, comes an understanding of the wholeness of life. When we speak of the relevance of the Buddha's teachings, it is futile to become trapped in debates over my '-yana' or your '-ism'. By letting ourselves be overpowered by a sense of self-righteousness, we begin to judge and condemn whatever does not fit into our limited framework.

I have attended gatherings on Buddhist studies at which it is hard to imagine that people are talking of the same great teacher; each 'unseeing one' clings to his or her part of the elephant whether a tail, a leg or a trunk firmly declaring that that limb alone is the whole creature! A sense of humour, a gift of laughter will not allow you to do this, because your sense of proportion allows you to see things in their proper perspective. It also allows room for views that seem to differ from your own. The gift of laughter seems to originate, according to Trungpa, in an all-pervading joy, a joy that has the space to expand into a completely open situation because it is not involved with the battle between 'this' and 'that'. This is a joy that develops, for the individual, into the panoramic situation of seeing or feeling the whole ground, the open ground. A person with a sense of humour cannot but be compassionate in his or her heart. It will be seen, then, that a sense of humour and compassion are both born from an understanding of greater connections, from an insight into the interrelatedness of all things and all living beings.

Pathways to Peace & Happiness

Mata Amritanandamayi

Our god-given abilities are a treasure that is meant for ourselves as well as for the entire world. This wealth should never be misused and made into a burden for us and for others. The greatest tragedy in life is not death; it is to let our great potential, talents, and capabilities go underutilized. When we use the wealth obtained from nature, it diminishes; but when we use the wealth of our inner gifts, it increases.

Today, we search outwardly for the causes and solutions to all the problems of the world. In our haste, we forget the greatest truth of all — that the source of all problems is to be found within the human mind. We forget that the world can become good only if the mind of the individual becomes good. So, along with an understanding of the outer world, it is essential that we also get to know the inner world.

Love is our true essence. Love has no limitations such as religion, race, nationality, or caste. We are all beads strung together on the same thread of love. To awaken this unity and to spread the love that is our inherent nature to others — this is the true aim of human life. Indeed, love is the only religion that can help humanity rise to great and glorious heights. And love should be the one thread on which all religions and philosophies are strung together. The beauty of society lies in the unity of hearts. Communication through machines has made people in distant places seem very close. Yet, because of the lack of communication of our hearts, even those who are physically close to us can seem very far away.

Religion and spirituality are the keys with which we can open our hearts and see everyone with compassion. But our minds, being blinded by selfishness, have lost proper judgment; our vision has become distorted. And this attitude will only serve to create more darkness. Using that very same key that is meant to open our hearts, our indiscriminate mindset locks our hearts shut instead. In today's world, people experience two types of poverty; the poverty caused by lack of food, clothing, and shelter, and the poverty caused by lack of love and compassion. Of these two, the second type needs to be considered first — because, if we have love and compassion in our hearts, then we will wholeheartedly serve those who suffer from lack of food, clothing, and shelter. In order to protect this world, we have to choose a path by which we forsake our personal differences and desires. By forgiving and forgetting, we can try to recreate and give new life to this world. It is useless to dig up and scrutinize the past; it won't benefit anyone. We need to abandon the path of vengeance and retaliation, and impartially evaluate the present world situation. Only then can we discover the path to true progress.

The body will perish whether we work or sit idle. So instead of rusting away without doing anything for society, it is better to wear oneself out in the pursuit of good actions. Today's world needs people who express goodness in their words and deeds. If such noble role models can set an example for their fellow beings, the darkness now prevailing in society will be dispelled, and the light of peace and non-violence will once again illumine this earth. Let us work together towards this goal. Let us grow and unfold as one family, united in love so that we may rejoice and celebrate our oneness in a world where peace and contentment prevail.

Joy or Misery, you Choose

Dinesh Kumar

If we make responsible choices, we get satisfying results. Choice equals creation, says Gary Zukav, in *The Seat of the Soul* and *The Mind of the Soul*. We choose everything we do including misery, says William Glassner, the psychiatrist who wrote *Choice Theory*.

Other people can make us neither miserable nor happy. All we can get from them or give them is information. But by itself, information cannot make us do anything or feel anything. It goes into our brain where we process it and then decide what to do. Therefore, we are very much in control of our lives than we believe. Zukav takes this concept to a sublime level when he says that most people think their experiences show them that they are not what they have chosen. They do not know that they have the ability to shape their experiences like a potter shapes clay. You are the artist and you are also the art that is being created. You choose the colours, where to add and remove clay and you choose whether the art is dark and depressing or light and joyful. If there are any limits to this, these are self-imposed. And yet the most common refrain in our society is 'I am miserable' or 'You make me so mad that I can't think straight'. It never crosses our minds that we are choosing the misery we are complaining about. And the misery will keep coming to us until we see clearly that our experiences of misery are consequences of our choices and choose differently to get rid of something that we do not like.

Why does such a simple concept not find universal acceptance? The reason, I suspect, is that the role of a victim is so attractive that we get hooked to it. The cost of being a complaining victim has a corresponding pay-off and that pay-off is the attention we get from our friends and relatives. We get used to hearing and liking the expression 'poor thing' and often the pain of coming out of the victim mould is greater than staying stuck. There is some degree of safety in sameness. The process of change is not easy but it is the heart of development.

In physical terms, we readily accept the cause and effect theory and Newton's law of action and reaction. But, in the laboratories of our lives, we discard the principle of cause and effect. In life's laboratory, cause goes to the intention level. "What effect will this intention cause?" is the question. And if we don't like the effect we have to try another intention.

If we accept the premise that we alone are responsible for making a choice, we have to accept total responsibility for the consequence our choice creates. If that choice creates a mess in our lives, we alone have to get down on our knees and clean that mess. Whether our choices are large ones concerning work, marriage and parenting, or small ones like getting edgy with a colleague, the responsibility will devolve on us.

William Glasser points out that we generally make responsible choices when we interact with our friends, bosses and strangers but when it comes to our families, the concept of ownership creeps in. I own my wife and therefore I can impose a choice that I believe will work for us. That is a cause of misery. A responsible choicemaker believes that as much as he has the right of making his choices and facing the consequences, others too have the same right. One question continues to haunt me: Does a person living in severe poverty or suffering from an untreatable illness or one who is in the depth of depression have such clear choices? I am still dealing with that doubt.

Success & Joy: The Difference

Geet Sethi

Morpheus says in *The Matrix*: "There's a difference between knowing the path, and walking the path." Life is not easy, packed as it is with challenges. And in the process of living, we feverishly pursue success, joy and happiness, believing in our hearts that they are interlinked, that one leads to the other in a smooth flow. But it's a mirage that constantly eludes us. Joy is often misunderstood; it is also easily forgotten. Yet, the optimum quality of life as we recognize it, is realized through these moments of joy. Joy is the ultimate but to experience it, you have to be yourself. The lightness of joy is like a feather, free falling in the wind and slipping through your fingers. Joy is internal, experienced through a culmination of perfect alignment, rhythm and timing of the self. This near-perfect synchronization leading to joy in its purest form is known as the 'sweet spot'.

There is joy in any activity that leads to personal growth and excellence. It calls for enthusiasm (entheos, the God in you) that disregards successes and failures. When you realize your 'sweet spot' and know what you want, pursue it with a single-mindedness to the exclusion of all else. The 'sweet spot' is what drives you. In every game, the player needs to focus, align his mind, body and spirit. He cannot afford to let his attention waver. The road to excellence is paved with joy. But the path can get clouded over by lethargy, lack of courage, fear of failure and insecurities. These invisible enemies are demons of the mind. Self-created, these demons break down the alignment of mind, body and spirit. It is crucial to recognize and then obliterate them from the mind. Use every cell in your body and brain to hit that personal 'sweet spot' of joy. Joy is internal whereas success is a creation of society.

Many a lifetime is spent in frustration, because most equate success with joy. But mere fame and money do not bring joy. Joy emanates from our own actions, from what one feels deep down inside. Success is a social concept measured by fame, money and power — don't fall into the trap. Success is said to be the consequence of certain actions, a result. The cause of the result called success is termed 'pure action' by Swami Parthasarathy in *The Vedanta Treatise*. Pure action has three qualities, concentration, consistency and cooperative endeavour. Concentration is defined as the intellect supervising the mind to remain in the present. The mind has to be continuously supervised as it travels back and forth — to the past and future — with equal velocity. An unleashed mind can cause self-destruction. An unwavering mind is the ultimate power of concentration.

A detached approach is beneficial. It helps you focus. Humility is another essential factor. It is important to recognize the contribution of parents, spouse, children and friends who have, over the years, relentlessly given their love, support and attention. On your part, you have to sacrifice everything except the 'passion' and your family. There is no room for a third. Eventually, the spirit within is reality for it's the soul that matters, not the external environment. Pursue the truth and do not deviate from your chosen path. Do not give up without a struggle. Do not quit unless you have stretched your potential to its limits. Only then will you experience the joy that makes life worth living. This is the joy that underscores success. Commitment to joy will create it's own success. Seek joy and success will naturally follow.

Life is Celebration, be Happy

Shashin

All of us want to be happy. Mystics say happiness is our nature. Happiness cannot be created and all that is needed to be happy is to be alive. Yet the whole world is miserable. Material wealth cannot make us happy and the richest society is facing the vulnerabilities of modern life. Yet, in our search for happiness, we constantly grope for sources in the outside world.

Osho says, "A happy person is not one who is always happy. He is happy even when there is unhappiness. Happiness is not conditional. The thumb rule is, to have happiness in you. Happiness alone can welcome and accept happiness... There are two ways to live life: outwards in search of happiness and inwards in search of bliss. Bliss wells up from your own sources, hence it is impossible to lose it." Our mind searches for happiness but the nature of human mind is to be on the move. And in our search we miss many moments to live happily.

Once a rich man wanted to be happy. He was in search of a wise man who could guide him on how to be happy. Some villagers assured him that a Sufi mystic who lived in the forest would be able to help him. The man found the mystic sitting peacefully below a tree. He stopped his horse and told him that he was unhappy. The mystic said that to find happiness he would have to hand over his jewels. The man gave him a bag of diamonds. Taking the jewel bag the mystic ran away. Thinking that he had been robbed, the man chased the mystic but failed to catch him. Desperate for his diamonds he returned to the forest. To his surprise he found the master sat in silence with his eyes closed at the same spot and the bag lay in front of him. Grabbing it, he danced with joy. The mystic opened his eyes and asked the man if he was happy to recover his riches. The man fell at his feet. The master added, "You have to know suffering; only then you know what happiness is."

Osho suggests a meditation technique. He says, "When you are unhappy visualize happiness. Similarly when you are happy visualize unhappiness. Slowly the opposite state absorbs the other." Once you understand your sadness, it disappears. This technique can transform you because "happiness is here and now... When you are free both from pain and pleasure, good and bad, light and darkness, life and death, when you are free from all dualities — that state, that transcendence, is *moksha*."

Also we should be happy in others' happiness. This way, we can experience instant joy. However, we must not stop and hoard happiness. Rather we should share it like the flowers share their scent with the winds. In dark and dismal moments we must build trust and happiness within us. We should start our day with a suggestion that life is a gift, that irrespective of what happens we will be happy and we will celebrate. We should search our inner source of happiness.

"Be happy, respect happiness, and help people to understand that happiness is the goal of life — *sat-chit-ananda*. The Eastern mystics have said God has three qualities. He is *sat*: he is truth, being. He is *chit*: consciousness, awareness. And, ultimately, the highest peak is *ananda*: bliss. Wherever bliss is, God is. Whenever you see a blissful person, respect him, he is holy. And wherever you feel a gathering which is blissful, festive, think of it as a sacred place," says Osho. Sorrow depletes the vitality of life, while joy makes us alive. So don't hanker for happiness; rather, search for bliss. That's what meditation is all about — the technology of the inner search for the eternal in you.

Attain Peace & Joy: Change yourself

Sadhguru Jaggi Vasudev

We are all subject to conflict and pain because people believe in different things — what is real for some is unreal for others. Naturally, conflict cannot be avoided. When each believes that only his way is right, people are bound to fight.

All religions started as instruments to find the inward path. But over time, they have undergone many changes and become different sets of beliefs. Though all religions speak of the value of human life, for the sake of the same religions, today people are willing to take each other's lives. Much pain and conflict has increased on earth because of this. This basic problem has not been properly addressed. People are always trying to do 'patch up' jobs — between individual and between groups, but these solutions do not last for long. This is because people believe in something which is not yet a reality for them. If you come down to reality, it is the same reality for everybody, no matter what religious background you come from. When you come to belief, each group has its own belief of what is right and what is wrong, what is true and false. You believe in things that you have not seen and experienced. This has become the basis of all conflict.

The basic purpose of yoga has always been to pursue religion as an inner experience, not as a belief. Don't start with any belief; start looking inward. Whatever is true, experience it and go further, approach it as a science. In yoga, we ensure that fundamentally a human being can grow or reach his Ultimate Nature, God or the Divine, or whatever you call it, by approaching it either through the body, the mind, emotion, or through inner energies. These are the only four realities that you know. Everything else is imagined. Everything else has been taught to you. These are the four basic ways of yoga. If the body is used for growth, it is Karma yoga. If the mind or intelligence is used, it is Gnana yoga. If emotion — love and devotion are used, then it is Bhakti yoga. If you transform your energies and grow, it is Kriya yoga. This is like referring to head, heart, hands and energy. That's what you are; that's what every human being is. Nobody is all head, or all heart, or all hands, or all energy, they are a combination of these four dimensions. So, if a person has to grow, he needs a combination of these four paths of Bhakti, Gnana, Kriya and Karma. Spiritually, there is nothing happening. Unless something of true value happens within a person, nothing of tremendous value can be done in the external world. Whatever you do, it is only your quality that you are going to spread. Whether you like it or not, this is the reality.

Who you are is what you are going to spread everywhere. If you are concerned about the world, the first thing is, you must be willing to transform yourself. Yoga is about 'I am willing to change myself'. This is not about wanting to change the world — it is about your willingness to change. Only when you are willing to change, can a change really happen in this world. When you say, "I want everybody else to change," only conflict will occur. Only when you are willing to change will there be transformation. It is this self-transformation that will lead to true well-being for the individual and society. A true revolution.

Stress-free Action Brings Peace & Joy

Alok Chopra

Action is imperative for success and progress because otherwise, inactivity takes over and leads to devolution. Activity, however, can generate a lot of stress in the individual. Progress, therefore, is risky. When progress is gained at the expense of peace of mind, it comes to lose its significance, because it does not translate into giving happiness. And to achieve happiness is the goal of all activity. So there's a dilemma: How does one be dynamic and still achieve peace of mind?

The *Bhagavad Gita* shows how we can move towards peace and joy even while remaining engaged in activity. It does not preach retirement from action. Swami Parthasarathy says, "The *Gita* is a skill for dynamic living; it is not a retirement plan. Most people try to get away from work in order to look for peace of mind. The *Gita* tells us that peace must be part of action, not divorced from it. The cause of stress is not activity but the attitude with which we approach work. Work approached rightly must itself be invigorating, joyful and rewarding." Stress is caused by several factors. Actions performed out of attachment cause stress. Such actions spring from selfishness and breed further selfish actions. Our whole attention is upon our own personal gain and satisfaction.

The aim is merely to cater to one's likes and dislikes. Right action ought to be based upon an ever-expanding unselfish goal. A goal higher than our present level of identification. In such a case the mind is restrained from getting attached. An employee's preoccupation must shift from personal benefits to that of the organization he works for. Once he is able to do so, he must shift his attention to benefiting the society or industry. Thus the mental horizon is allowed to broaden. Stress is caused when not sufficient room is given for the mind to expand. A mind bottled up in the confines of its attachments feels stifled and stressed.

Indulgence is another cause for stress. Within the field of our attachments we continuously generate desires which look for release. A mind pulsating with unfulfilled desires causes stress. In order to release ourselves from it we indulge in the senses. Overeating, unnecessary talking and indiscriminate shopping for example. This only aggravates the problem. So the vicious cycle continues. The remedy is to bring the indiscriminate thought flow under intellectual control. The contact with the world must be under the dictates of the intellect and not the mind. This arrests the multiplication of desires. The conserved energy must be directed to a higher ideal. Actions performed with an attitude of serving a higher purpose keep the mind cheerful and vibrant. The attitude of doership is another factor causing stress.

Innumerable factors contribute towards the success or failure of our actions. No person can have conscious control over them. An egoistic person functions without being aware of or acknowledging any law or power beyond himself. He wishes to bring the fruits of his actions within his control. He resists things going against his wishes or will. Such a rigid and non-accepting attitude is a fertile ground for stress. In order to counter this effect one must forsake the egoistic stand and surrender to the laws of nature. Whatever be one's merits one can never supersede the laws governing life. One can only understand and abide by them. A wise man is one who recognizes this truth and allows the forces of nature to supplement and not contradict his efforts. Actions cleansed of attachment and egoistic notions become a means of energy, cheer and progress.

Celebrating Bliss which is Brahman

Pravin Shanker Mehta

The teachings of t[...]sed on four noble truths, Arya Satya a[...]n. (1) Misery, *dukha*, All life is misery. Th[...] of being born under conditions of finite existence renders a living being, subject to sickness, old age, frustration of unfulfilled desires and finally a painful death. As the poet Tennyson says 'We are born in other's pain and perish in our own'. (2) Cause of misery is desire, *Trishna*. (3) Misery can be destroyed (4) The noble eightfold path of righteousness, is understanding, purpose, speech, conduct, vocation, effort, alertness and concentration, leads to cessation of misery. This is Nirvana where all misery is destroyed for ever. While referring to Nirvana, the Buddha avoids using the term *ananda*, bliss. Buddhist scholar Ashwaghosha has likened Nirvana to the extinguishing of the flame of a lamp. A flame is extinguished with the burning up of oil. It goes nowhere.

Similarly a *jiva* attaining Nirvana goes neither here nor there. With the annihilation of suffering, only peace remains. The Buddha always declined to enter upon a discussion on metaphysical speculations such as, world, soul, god, after-life etc. His disciple Maulikyaputta requested him to explain whether the creation was eternal or not, whether soul and body were one or different, whether the Tathagata existed after Nirvana and similar other subjects. The Buddha answered by citing example of a man lying grievously wounded with a poisonous arrow stuck in his chest. A doctor offers to extricate the arrow and ease his suffering. But the injured man refuses to have the arrow extricated from his body before knowing the name, caste, figure, vocation, place of residence etc. of the person who shot the arrow. In the meantime he continues to suffer and will surely die before he finds the answers to his questions. Similarly engaging oneself in metaphysical speculations is futile and does not help in anyway in the cessation of misery which happens only after

Nirvana is achieved. The primary objective therefore should be annihilation of misery. As regards metaphysical questions, the Buddha is just noncommital. His response is that of silence.

Sankara on the other hand has followed the positivism of the Upanishads by referring to the state of deliverance as Brahman or *ananda*, 'Anand Bramheti Vijanata' — *Ananda* is Brahman. The term *ananda*, bliss, is grossly misunderstood by the limited human mind which is incapable of comprehending any state beyond sensory perceptions. So the mind thinks of *ananda* as some highly intensified form of *sukha*, pleasure, may be a million times more intense, but basically some experience like pleasure. But as Osho says *ananda* is not like *sukha* at all. The difference between the two is not of degrees. The difference is qualitative, not quantitative. *Ananda* is not the experience of an individual at all. It is the state wherein the individual merges into the universal reality.

However, the misunderstood concept of *ananda* as intensified *sukha*, is very tempting to humankind. It appears worth striving for. The negativity of Nirvana does not enthuse the human mind as *ananda* does. Just as painful thorn pricking the body will be removed. Is that all? One feels let down as it were. As the poet Keats has sung 'Heard melodies are sweet, those unheard sweeter'. But unlike other sages the Buddha has purposely refrained from selling rosy dreams to the Human minds, as he knows that they would just be a mirage.

According to Osho, the reason for the respective negative and positive terminology used by the Buddha and Sankara can be traced to their respective lives. The Buddha was born a prince. His life was like the sundial which marks only the sunny hours. So his mind gravitated towards the dark side of life ie, the problem of misery and he offered a practical solution for the same. Sankara on the other hand was born in penury. His life was a tale of wants and struggles. So the concept of *ananda* attracted his mind.

Actually both the Buddha and Sankara are referring to the same state of deliverance from the painful unending cycle of births and deaths. The difference is only in their respective choice of terms. Nirvana and *ananda* are the two sides of the same coin. The metal is the same, only the outer engravings are different. No wonder Sankara has been called by some a 'Prachchanna Bauddha', a concealed Buddhist.

Bliss as the State beyond Happiness

Vijay T Salve

No living being is free from stress. Stress starts right from conception. In human beings it is perceived at 'cortical' level. Advances in science and technology has not made life easy but in fact added more stress. No wonder stress induced diseases like hypertension, coronary artery diseases, and many other psychosomatic diseases are on rise. The magnitude of stress differs from individual to individual and so the ability to cope up with the same. Stress is, in short, an unpleasant experience perceived mentally, giving a feeling of dissatisfaction and frustration. If one thinks over, it results out of the inability of an individual to accept the non-existence of 'imaginary idealism'. This imaginary idealism, so to say, is an ideology based on experience prejudices, assumptions and presumptions.

Modern science, including physics and medicine, has advanced to reason out and solve problems of humankind to some extent. But phenomenon of 'Randomness of occurrence' has made science crippled, limited. Each individual, every phenomenon, is unique in itself. As a medical man, I have experienced this randomness in the sense that in spite of the best of efforts, diseases do not get cured, the course of the disease gets variable and sometimes the patient dies in the best of hospitals. This abyss gives us our neurotic minds a 'nihilistic' view of life. The big 'why' cannot be answered every time and we tend to land up in the infinite loop of 'why' and 'how', which ultimately leads to frustration. Carl Jung, one of the pioneers of modern psychiatry and an associate of Sigmund Freud, has said, "Theories based on experience are essentially statistical, that it formulates an 'ideal average' which abolishes all exceptions on either ends of scale and replace them by imaginary mean. This mean is quite valid, though it may not exists in reality. Ultimate truth is the goal of science and this cannot be reached by our limited conscious experience."

In here comes the ultimate and supreme power, God, the only absolute entity. The power governing the universe. By realizing this fact one can break the infinite chain of unsolved queries. The limited human intellect cannot answer all questions and has to rely on the Supreme Lord. As Jung has truly said, "The rupture between knowledge and factor is a symptom of split consciousness, which is a characteristic of mental disorder of modern society."

Knowing the true nature of the self is an essential aspect in this context. The 'Inner Self' is not one's own body, mind thoughts, but it is that entity which is much beyond all this. In the *Bhagavad Gita*, it is said that one who conquers himself and his own self is a friend to himself, but to the unconquered 'self', this self appears like an external enemy. The Ashtavakra Samhita puts it differently: "Have faith my son, have faith. Never confuse yourself in this, you are knowledge itself, you are lord, you are self, much beyond, nature." By knowing the true nature of 'Inner Self', giving up false ego, one can definitely experience freedom from the psychic pattern of desire, frustration and depression. The 'Vipassana' technique of self observation was described by Gautam Buddha 2500 years ago.

One can learn this technique and just observe one's own thought and not necessarily act on them. The source of unhappiness in most instances is either past experience or future anticipation. One has to realize that the past has already happened and cannot be changed by any means and the future cannot be predicted. Living in the present is an essential key to happiness and a stress-free life. Discarding all prejudices, ideologies, presumptions and assumptions, living in the present moment and giving the credit of the final results to the Almighty, one can definitely experience bliss — a state that is beyond happiness.

Community Welfare & Individual Happiness

Bharat Dogra

Spiritual development helps reduce stress and expands our horizons, helping us experience a subliminal happiness that neither material riches nor relationships can yield. However, this spiritual development of the self is complete and meaningful only when it is related to the welfare of other people and other forms of life. Achievement of inner peace or deeper knowledge is not an end in itself. It becomes invaluable only when it is related to efforts for creating a better world.

How can we put ourselves in spiritual development mode? We should place voluntary restraints on the consumption of material goods so that our energies and capabilities can be released for higher forms of happiness derived from helping others. While it is necessary to know what we want, it is equally important to know what we don't want. Having met our basic needs and small comforts we should be in a position to say, "I don't want anything more. Now I would rather devote myself to helping others."

Just as we need to have clear views about the pleasures of life, similarly we need to have equally clear thinking about sorrow and how to face sorrow. Sorrow is an inevitable aspect of human life. The sources of sorrow, including extreme distress, are so many and so diverse that even the richest and the mightiest persons cannot buy or enforce immunity from sorrow. Sorrow being inevitable, we must be prepared to accept it with peace and patience. However, we should also be prepared to fight its causes with courage and tenacity, especially when distress is caused by the unjust acts of others.

When sorrow is caused by injustice, we should put up a resistance and fight. We should guard against becoming vindictive. While exercising control over sensual pleasures, it is important to overcome feelings of anger. Anger should give place to constructive action. Accepting the inevitability of distress also motivates us to develop those abilities which are likely to prove most helpful in times of distress — patience, the ability to think calmly, good health, and compassion. Times of distress can even be one of opportunity as it motivates us firstly to mobilize all our inner strengths to face adversity, and secondly, it strengthens our bonds and friendships. We emerge from adversity, not shattered and destroyed, but with a deeper ability to love one another and a stronger desire to resist injustice.

Anyone who wants to tread the path of spiritual development should bring his individual life into harmony with the requirements of community welfare, making an effort to understand the requirements of the people around us. Most relationships that exist in the present day world are relationships of dominance as persons, groups and nations try to get a better deal for themselves without bothering about the needs of others. There is an almost instinctive urge to dominate, by getting more resources, income and wealth for oneself at the cost of depriving others. Even when greed is not involved, there is still a strong desire to impose one's own views. These attitudes also spill over beyond human relations to our relationships with other forms of life and with nature. Anyone who has got used to dominating relationships also reduces himself or herself to a level of insensitivity which prevents him or her from experiencing many small but precious joys of life. This can erode and eventually even destroy invaluable relationships causing a lot of distress.

The urge to dominate others also denies an opportunity to calmly consider other points of view, thereby increasing the chances of making costly mistakes. Both to avoid causing great distress to others and to prevent grave self-harm the person who wants to tread the path of spiritual development should seek to avoid the trait of dominance and competitiveness in all relationships, and instead replace this with cooperation and coexistence.

One who walks the path of spiritual development should have the courage to stand up against the perpetrators of injustice. Extending a helping hand results in a happiness that is far above and superior to the 'happiness' we get from pursuing self-interest. When we voluntarily prepare ourselves to make sacrifices that include the risk of suffering deprivation, disease, injury and even death for the sake of removing injustice and suffering, happiness comes to us automatically. However, the basic motive for choosing this path is not to achieve individual happiness but the creation of a better world.

The Gateway to Bliss

Jaya Row

Meditation is the highest spiritual technique that needs to be practised diligently and devotedly by qualified practitioners. The essential prerequisite is a calm mind. A mind burdened with desires and attachments is unable to take off into subtler realms of concentration and meditation. Entitled 'The Yoga of Meditation', chapter 6 of the *Bhagavad Gita* elucidates meditation as the final gateway to Self-realization. Krishna begins with the definition of a *sannyasi*, a renounced person. Renunciation is not giving up enjoyments, abandoning one's duties and escaping to a safe sanctuary.

It is this misunderstanding that has turned away genuine seekers and prevented them from accessing the benefits of renunciation. Krishna describes a *sannyasi* as one who does what one ought to do, fulfils one's duties and responsibilities fully, without depending on the fruit of action. A *sannyasi* is not one without a higher ideal, nor is he an inactive person. Krishna describes the three stages of spiritual evolution, from an active *yogi* to a meditative *sannyasi* and, finally, to the exalted state of a *jnani*, the enlightened One.

A *sannyasi* has offloaded the bulk of his desires and is in contemplation of the higher. He is fit for meditation and embarks on the path of deep reflection and focus on reality. A *jnani* has reached the exalted state of enlightenment. Krishna describes the three stages in terms of mental states rather than external appearances. Thus, one does not have to don ochre robes or perform rituals or deny oneself worldly enjoyments to be spiritual. All that is needed is a change in mindset. Step by step, Krishna takes us through the preparatory disciplines as well as disqualifications for meditation.

One must have a balanced contact with the world — neither too much nor too little. Every activity must be carefully supervised by the intellect so that no desire interrupts the subtle practise of meditation. If the contact with the world is excessive the mind is rushing out to the world and is unable to concentrate. Meditation is a far cry. If one shies away from worldly enjoyment one only succeeds in getting frustrated. Such people are also unfit for meditation. Krishna then gives the test of enlightenment.

A realized soul is one who feels one with everyone. He sees his Self as the Self in all beings. In the end he worships God not in a temple, church or mosque, but in every living being. Thereafter he lives in *atman*, whatever his lifestyle. It is pointless to declare love for God when you cannot connect with His images everywhere. Arjuna, like us, is afraid of leaving the safe confines of his present existence to discover the unknown realm of the Infinite. He asks Krishna what the fate is of those who commit themselves to a spiritual life but die before realization.

Krishna gives a fitting reply to reveal one of the most insightful laws of life. He says, "One who is righteous will never come to grief — either now or in the future." Your efforts will not go in vain. You will carry forward the credits to your future life. A spiritually evolved person who falls short of realization will either be born in the home of the happy and wealthy or in a family of wise *yogis*. There, endowed with the wisdom acquired in previous lives, he will strive even more to attain enlightenment.

Lakshmi's Lotus of Perfect Happiness

KM Gupta

The Sri Suktam in the Rig Veda is a hymn to Lakshmi, the goddess of wealth. She is lotus-born and lotus-dwelling. She holds lotuses in her hands. She wears lotus garlands. She is lotus-eyed. She is lotus all over. In Greek thought the lotus suggests indolent happiness; in Indian philosophy the lotus stands for perfection. The lotus-holding and lotus-dwelling Lakshmi is the symbol of perfect happiness. The Sri Suktam verses praise Lakshmi as the *deva-vanita* and asks her, "Dost thou worship me? — *twam mam bhajaswa*? Your worship of me would get me perfect happiness — *yena soukhyam labhamyaham*. What, indeed, is happiness? After deep thought we find that happiness is mobility. In contrast, misery is lack of mobility. We are happy to the extent that we are mobile; we are miserable in proportion to our immobility. To get happiness, things have to go our way. For things to go our way, the lie of the land should be favourably inclined to us.

Phenomenal existence is a four-dimensional space-time-consciousness continuum (FDSTCC) that we call luck, lot, fate, karma, fortune, providence, destiny, grace, god, and all. Whatever is there beyond our knowledge and control in space, time and consciousness, whatever we call it, it is actually the FDSTCC geometry. That is the science of God and karma. Work and worship are the two means in man's hand to turn the FDSTCC geometry favourably inclined towards himself. Because of the infinite pulls and pressures on it from infinite quarters, the FDSTCC geometry is almost always hostile. To work out a favourable inclination we have to work and worship harder and harder. Work is in our hand. We can work to the best of our ability. But there is no guarantee work alone would do the trick. Sometimes even the hardest and most sincere work bears no fruit; sometimes even Herculean efforts go down the drain.

Even after all the slogging, one needs the favour of Lady Luck. She is the figuration of a favourable inclination of the FDSTCC geometry.

Lakshmi is the Christian name of Lady Luck. Sanatana Dharma sets out four *purusharthas* — dharma, *artha, kama, moksha.* The second, *artha,* is the pursuit of money. Without *artha* the other three do not move. Even *moksha* takes money, especially in this modern age. So money calls for worship. Rightly, Lakshmi is worshipped as the goddess of wealth. We don't worship her enough — this accounts for the so-called 'Hindu rate of growth', commonly attributed to a lack of the killer instinct. It might be a good idea to worship our philosophy-spewing male-gods less and devote more attention to the Lotus Lady. Lakshmi personifies not just money but the whole concept of prosperity and well-being. Money is just one petal of the lotus of perfect happiness. The lotus has eight petals of perfect happiness and hence we have Ashta Lakshmi — *Dhana, Dhanya, Santana, Dhairya, Vidya, Vijaya, Aishwarya* and *Vaibhava* Lakshmis. All the eight Lakshmis have to get together to make for perfect happiness. However, the 'Moolah' Lakshmi or Dhana Lakshmi is the 'first among equals' and she can make up for the other Lakshmis to a large extent.

It is as hard to keep Lakshmi as to win her favour. She walks out on one who takes her for granted, even if it is her spouse. Bhrigu the *rishi* once set out on a mission to find out who among the Trimurtis is the best. He ran riot in their houses. In Brahmaloka he cursed Brahma the creator to lose out shrines and worship on earth; in Kailasa he cursed Shiva to be worshipped not in his own form but in the form of the phallus because at the time of Bhrigu's visit Shiva was engrossed in his spouse Parvati. In Vaikunta he found Vishnu and Lakshmi together and he kicked at the Lord's chest. Vishnu didn't take Bhrigu's bad behaviour to heart. He forgave the insolent *rishi.* He even expressed concern that the *rishi* might have hurt his foot. Lakshmi, however, didn't take kindly to the insult. Nor did she approve of her husband's lenient attitude. She rose in revolt to the extent of declaring that the bond of mutual obligation, *rinanubandha,* the knot, between her and the lord is now cut, and threatened to leave Vaikunta for good. O ye the proud Lotus Lady, I worship you in order that I can get you to worship me. Happiness flows not out of my worship of you, but from your worship of me.

Happiness through Head & Heart

Dada JP Vaswani

Thoughts dodge you. Questions storm you. And you are lost in the jigsaw puzzle of queries and more queries. The question that troubles most rational human beings is, 'Why am I born?' My humble answer to that is the one given by Buddha, The Enlightened one, to his disciples: When the house is on fire, first extinguish it with water. Don't just stand there in front of the burning house and reason out the cause of it. The cause would be known only when the fire is put out. Similarly, now that you are born and are living on this planet Earth, you must live in the manner which is most positive. For that you have to work hard.

Treat life not as an imposition but as a gift from God — to be loved and to be cherished. Move on the pathway of life with faith and courage, and the confidence that he is with you. Accept life with all its trials and tribulations. Acceptance of whatever is, will solve half of your problems. Know that whatever your life is today, is your own making. It is the combined result of your karma, in the previous birth and the exercise of your 'free will' before you were born in this life. You yourself have shaped your life, for your own good. So my mantra is: Accept your life with all its trials and suffering.

What do you seek in your day-to-day living? Happiness! How many have experienced happiness? How many can define happiness? Yet everyone seeks happiness. That's ultimate goal. Few know where to seek happiness. Most of you seek happiness outside of yourselves. You run after money, power, wealth, authority, status, name and fame. You are running after the shadows of happiness. True happiness comes from within, from the purification of mind and the ultimate intuition of heart.

Yes, there arises a question. Should you listen to the voice of the head or the voice of the heart? My answer is simple. Listen to the voice of the heart through the head. Emotions lead us astray. We need head as much as we need heart. Develop both to an extent where both converge to a point of light, and your goal of happiness is achieved.

People are awed by the miracles of science as much as they are fascinated by the powers of spirituality. There is no competition between the two. Science is the discovery of one area and spirituality is the discovery of another area; in the final analysis there is no difference, both are discoveries, both are an experience of an 'awareness'. Our *rishis* had this knowledge. They had gained the knowledge of science through intuition. So where is the difference? As the New Age dawns, materialism will automatically lag behind spirituality. And people will live the Vedanta in their daily lives. The Vedantic concept is spiritual. One life flows in all things. Therefore the future civilization will be built on reverence for life. All life is sacred. Therefore in your day-to-day living, show reverence for everything: the earth, the sky, the trees, stones, rivers, animals, flowers. The Vedantic concept is spiritual but it is one which is scientific, for scientists tell us that there is life even in a stone and that the molecules in a stone are ever changing. Now the time has come when man must either make friends with Nature or perish. This is the Truth.

Religion is life; it is fellowship, the mingling of the individual with the Great Life. And it is not shut up in temples, it is moving in the market place. The great God is not somewhere in isolation. He is in the procession of life. Greet Him there! You will not find him in the temples of marbles and stones, you will meet Him in the sweat and struggle of life, in the tears and tragedies of the poor; wiping the tears of the poor and singing his new *Gita* for the New Age! So if you want to be happy make others happy.

Yes, my vision of life is secularistic. Secularistic in the spiritual sense and not the religious sense. The spirit of humanity is One. In this life we have to work for the unity of mankind. The coming civilization will be built on a nobler thought, and that thought is, 'You are Me. I am You'. In that oneness, Joy, Peace and Love will grow.

Feeling Blissful is only the Beginning

Sadhguru

The moment I say "spirituality" people say, "Yes, I want to be peaceful." If you take a long walk and lie down, you will sleep peacefully. If you eat a good dinner, you will sleep peacefully. You don't need the spiritual process to be peaceful. The longing for peace has essentially come from troubled minds of those who are torturing themselves — for them, peace is a big commodity that they have to seek. If you are not using your mind for self-torture, why would you think of peace? Would you seek exuberance of life or would you seek peace?

You 'rest in peace'. If you want to be peaceful, you must be dead. Now is the time to live. But for those who have lost control over their mental faculty what should have been a miracle has become a misery-manufacturing machine. Even being ecstatic is not a goal by itself. If you are blissful by your own nature, then the important thing is, you are not the issue anymore. If you are an issue yourself, what other issue will you take into your hands? You will not touch anything. When you are no more an issue, then you are willing to plumb the whole of existence to know what it is all about.

Mysticism evolved only in those places where people learnt the technology of being ecstatic by their own nature. For you to experience a little bit of pleasantness within you, if you have to drink, dance, or do something crazy, you will never explore other dimensions of life because keeping yourself pleasant itself is a great challenge and a full-time job. For most, the pursuit of happiness has become the goal of life. Happiness is not something you achieve. It is something that you start with; it is the square one of life. As children, we all started joyfully without any hassle. So, do not understand the spiritual process as one of peace, joy or even bliss. Only if you are blissful, you will truly explore all aspects of life.

There was a time when we believed that whether the tree in our garden bears fruit or not depended on God's will. But we took charge of these things. Now we know if this tree is not bearing fruit what the problem is. We know what to do. So, when you understand that if your Self has not blossomed, it has got nothing to do with anything except that you are not doing the right thing with yourself. Once we understand that, the spiritual process actually begins.

Once you are not an issue, being peaceful, joyful or blissful is not an effort anymore; then naturally you want to know what is behind everything. This is not an induced quest, seeking comes naturally. The spiritual process is not a conscious choice; it is a kind of compulsive behaviour. But unless you handle it consciously, it will not yield. Longing for the boundless is compulsive, but unless you become conscious, it will never work.

If you want to know, experience and handle other dimensions, it is important that you have no rigid structures in your mind. The biggest thing in existence is not a god sitting somewhere. The life process itself contains the creation and the Creator. If you are willing to go beyond the surface substance of what you call yourself, suddenly everything is malleable. Here and There, Now and Then all merge. The individual and the universal are different no more. Unless one experiences the universality of one's nature, human form is wasted. To eat, sleep, reproduce and die, you do not need a human body, intelligence and awareness. Every worm or insect can fulfil that better than a human being.

Think Positive to be Pain-free & Happy

Mahi Pal

Most people expect fruits of an action in terms of expectations before initiating any action or performing duties. If we follow the dictum that we have performed our duties earnestly and the outcome is not in our hands, then the pain will not be experienced because at that time the mind would be in a state of wantlessness.

Each one of us has wants. We expect to satisfy these wants in order to experience happiness in our daily lives. One want creates a number of wants. When these wants remain unfulfilled or partly fulfilled, they create unhappiness and the more we think about it, the more miserable we feel. This way, we only inflict pain on ourselves. Could this way of life be sustainable in the present context where people are surrounded with different kinds of stress-creating situations?

How does one find happiness in the midst of so much greed, anxiety and dissatisfaction? Real happiness does not come by creating wants; it can only come through slowly reducing or even eliminating them. Pain and happiness are two sides of the same coin. If you are capable of feeling pain, definitely there is the possibility of feeling happiness. But true progress is made only when you learn to rise above both pain and pleasure, happiness and sadness. The remedy lies in keeping yourself away from the state of pain and pleasure.

You can avoid or keep away from both pain and pleasure only when you willingly lose your so-called individuality to embrace universality. This is only possible if people do not have desires and their motive of taking up activities is to reach a state of wantlessness. This does not, however, mean that running a business or working to earn money is a bad thing or is totally unnecessary. What is limiting — what prevents you from seeking higher realms —

is the persistent desire in you to acquire more and more that in turn even more wants. It's a never-ending spiral.

Constant recollection of negative events could also be avoided to achieve a pain-free state. In the sea, there are disturbances only on the surface; deep inside, there is tranquillity. This approach to life — of remaining calm despite turbulence outside — could help us overcome suffering. The moment a want arises, an attempt is also made to satisfy it. Fulfilling a want gives satisfaction and pleasure because not doing so is unacceptable. In this process we are constantly engaged in endlessly creating wants and fulfilling them. Conversely, satisfying a want means yielding to it, becoming enslaved by it.

But this cycle does not create enduring happiness because this is an unending process. The best way of getting sustainable state of satisfaction is not to yield to a want but to eliminate a want instead of obeying its dictations. Hence, instead of satisfying a want which is a continuous process, it is always better to overcome it. The best way is to replace all your myriad wants with just one worthy desire — the desire or want to find the Supreme Truth. In pursuit of this all-encompassing desire, everything else drops off. With practice and devotion, the seeker reaches a stage when all that matters is making the goal of self-realization attainable. Once the Truth dawns on the seeker, finally, the state of wantlessness is achieved and there is no more pain. No more suffering. Only a state of perfect happiness or bliss.

Yogic Steps to Achieve Success & Happiness

Swami Kriyananda

When we say, "Be practical", what do we mean? Unfortunately, the common understanding of what is practical is reflected in the attitude that says, "A chasm yawns between idealism and reality. You can have your ideals, but don't relate them to business matters, or to getting things done in the real world."

Realpolitik is an expression invented in Germany for politics based on a hard-headed and cynical attitude towards 'reality' — a narrow perception. It is this kind of approach that gives a handle for unethical and inhuman behaviour that disregards the importance of compassion, brotherhood and oneness. 'Practicality' has been waved like a banner to declare that spirituality and high ideals belong in the temple, mosque and church, but not in the 'real' world of business. Hard-headed business practices are perceived too often as having nothing to do with ideals: they are purely a matter of making money. Into this thinking there creeps very easily the consciousness that dishonesty in business is perfectly justifiable — the sort of consciousness that justifies itself by saying, "One can't make an omelette without breaking a few eggs."

In such an environment, a businessman who wishes to live by higher principles could face serious challenges. It was voiced to me recently by a doctor friend in India. "I believe in high principles," he said to me earnestly. "Practically speaking, however, how can I follow them? Life makes demands of me that I simply cannot meet unless, occasionally, I cut a few corners ethically. I have a son to put through college. I want to live by dharmic principles, but if I did so always I couldn't survive." It was that question which inspired me to write a course of lessons with the theme: 'Success and Happiness Through Yoga Principles'. My personal experience has been just the opposite: To live determinedly by high principles is the surest road to material security, and beyond that, to glowing material success. My hope is to convince all that by giving high ideals the highest priority in life, you could succeed far better at anything you try than if you think — in the name of a practicality — that by cheating someone today, one has made profit and so needn't worry about tomorrow.

The solution to the friend's question depends first of all on another simple question: What is the so-called practical approach doing for you? The friend's face showed some signs of his inner conflict. The truth is, when people 'cut corners' ethically, they cannot help creating a Kurukshetra-like inner war which pits the two selves within — the higher and the lower — in heated combat. A more hard-headed materialist might say, "What nonsense! I feel no such anguish!" That is because he has surrendered to the pull of his lower self. Let him ask himself then, instead, "Am I happy?" It is unlikely that he would say "yes".

It is a mistake to equate practicality with greed. One might prevaricate to obtain an unfair advantage over someone; or to cheat a customer by selling him a product one knows to be defective; or to damage a competitor's reputation by belittling his products and services. The truth is, honesty is the best policy.

Find the Right Track to Achieve Bliss

Sonam Tsomo

The core of all religious philosophies dwells on understanding the purpose and meaning of life. Understanding is at the root of development that leads one to ultimate deliverance or nirvana. Gifted as we are with intelligence, we should try to understand everything we have to deal with in our day-to-day life. It is important because a lack of understanding is the root cause of all that dogs us today.

According to the Buddha, understanding has two layers, *anubodhi* and *pativedha*. *Anubodhi* is what we call 'knowledge'. It is nothing but accumulated memory, an understanding of a particular subject on the basis of data or observation. It is, therefore, superficial. Real understanding comes from *pativedha* or deep penetration into the core of a subject. It enables us to understand an object in its true nature and colour. In it, all the exterior labels like name, fame, money and power have zero value. This kind of understanding can be developed only through rigid training of mind through meditation. One has to strive to be, first of all, free from all kinds of impurities that tend to derail us from the right path.

A person, on reaching this stage of penetrative wisdom, can see everything in the right perspective. He acquires the capability to make a distinction between what is desirable and correct and what is undesirable and incorrect. Such a person also develops the ability to acquire habits that enable his mind to see and believe nothing but the good of all.

The Buddha's philosophy of life revolves around the purification of mind and giving us deliverance from worldly attachments. The Buddha says every human being has the innate qualities and ability to come out of the world of ignorance and move towards the world of enlightenment. In other words, we have the choice. Until we try ourselves to get rid of the 'shackles of misery', no divine power can come to our rescue. Our gurus can only show us the way, but the real 'action' is in our hands. Therefore, the Buddha presented the path of *sila* or ethical conduct, *samadhi* or *meditation* and *panna* or wisdom as the means to purify the mind. These are quite often referred to as the threefold training or *tividhasikkha* system; but none of these is an end in itself. Each one is only a means to an end. And these three means go together. *Sila* strengthens one's mental discipline. So does *samadhi*. And the two lead to *panna*. It is wisdom that differentiates us from other life forms. It enables us to see life as it is, arising and passing away. The materialistic world has too many temptations. Our desire for fame, name, wealth and power has led us far away from the path of deliverance. Hatred, distrust and violence is the outcome of the lack of understanding of life. Our love for the gratification of senses has led to our experiencing bankruptcy of mind. However, a little more determination can still put us on to the right path. The Buddha's Eightfold Path can help us realize our objectives. The path to deliverance is difficult only for those who avoid it. Constant heedfulness and mindfulness can make the path easy to track. These practices are a way of life, and not just an 'add-on' to life. Those who try to live life through moral, spiritual and intellectual perfection are the ones who will be the ultimate reapers of happiness and bliss. Self-discipline in body, mind and word go a long way in helping one get closer to reality of life.

Let's overcome Stress as Children of Bliss

Swami Vishvas

The mind is compared to a monkey drunk with the wine of desire, stung by the scorpion of jealousy and possessed with the demon of pride. Lust, greed, jealousy, anger, ego, tensions, reactions, grudges, depression, stress and strain are the symptoms and not the disease. When we are afflicted with a disease like malaria, we don't treat each symptom like fever, pain and shivering, one by one. We just treat the disease and the symptoms automatically vanish. So deal directly with the mind and the symptoms of stress and strain will disappear.

Vishvas meditation is mind management. There is no attempt, however, to control the mind; the idea is to go beyond it. The common misconception is that meditation is concentration of mind and techniques are taught to achieve this. Meditation has got no technique. There are techniques for concentration. Concentration is a mental exercise between the mind and the object of attention. But meditation is neither a mental exercise nor a practice. Meditation is a direct and natural process beyond mind itself. Meditation is not concentration; it is the mother of concentration. Remember, concentration is where one tries to control the thoughts. Meditation is where thoughts get dissolved naturally, enhancing your concentration power, memory power, will-power, right thinking and fitness power automatically.

When thought current is interrupted which means that all the thoughts are fixed on one object, it is concentration. But when the flow is uninterrupted which means that the thought is not fixed on any one object, rather we just remain a non-doer and directly watch the thoughts as a neutral energy, without any judgment, analyses, participation, visualization, imagination, contemplation, suppression, repression, condemnation or concentration. That is meditation. Meditation is a non-doing entity where you are simply a seer, witness, an observer of the mind's happenings. To watch is our true nature. It is a natural, non-doing state. No effort is required to watch. We all have full potential to look within directly as we all are blessed with the 'Third Eye'.

Meditation is mind-management. It is not forcing the mind to be quiet. It is to find the quiet that is there already. We are children of bliss. We suffer from stress and strain because we gave all the powers to the mind and made it our master. Not only that, we consider ourselves nothing but the mind. Mind is matter. It has no power of its own. It is useful in the external world but in the spiritual, internal world, it has to be left far behind. Otherwise we will be the victim of mental and heart diseases. Meditation is seeing the mind as a witness, a neutral energy. It is not interfering with the intricacies and doings of mind. Let the mind go into the dead past or uncertain future in meditation. Just be a seer, be a witness. We just stay in our own source, in our true nature: All-bliss.

We are happy when the mind is cheerful. We are depressed when mind is gloomy. We are at the mercy of the mind that waxes and wanes. We consider ourselves nothing but mind. It is very unfortunate and a great blasphemy to consider ourselves as the victims of some unforeseen incident when the unending BLISS is flowing within all of us. Meditation is mind-management. Meditation is homecoming.

Happiness doesn't Happen to Us, it Happens by Us

Marguerite Theophil

When we look at people around us who have had relatively smooth and trouble-free lives, we find that some are happy, others unhappy. When we look at those who have had really rough and challenging lives, again, some are happy, others are not. All this seems to suggest the relevance of an age-old truth: happiness has less to do with circumstances than with our attitude and approach to life.

Happiness does not happen to us, it happens by us. Know that each of us is the creator of our own thoughts and state of mind. This does not mean ignoring the often, painful reality of what happens, but understanding that you can choose your response to something at any given moment. For example, you can choose to be frazzled and furious with the demands and pressures of a hectic day, feeling miserable about bad luck, colleagues, weather or bad whatever. Or you can call upon the grace of the moment — reminding yourself to stop and breathe calmly for just a few moments, finding some beauty to focus on, something to be grateful for in all this. You can choose between forever brooding on an unhappy childhood, or focusing on healing and moving on.

Happiness is called upon and cultivated, involving unlearning as much as learning. Consider that for a lot of people, unhappiness can be a 'patterned response'; where we choose a familiar emotional place even if it mostly hurts and brings sorrow. It's a bit like shadow, my friend's rescued puppy; a bruised, starving, sick little creature, he was given a loving caring home and owners. But after all this time, he still twitches, jumps, and scuttles away at the slightest sound or sudden movement. Shadow doesn't run and hide so much because he has something to be terrified of today but simply because that's what he has always done.

Experiences from early life can create habits and patterns that become deeply ingrained, influencing our moods and choices. But, unlike that miserable little dog, we do have the capacity to replace acquired fear or sadness with learned happiness. We can realize that blaming the past or others for our misery, even if partially true, can only give us excuses; it cannot give us the happiness we crave inside. In fact, it usually serves to increase our suffering! It is established that cultivating feelings of happiness results in a self-generating cycle of biological as much as psychological well-being. When you carve out time to go for a walk, or just to the nearest window, or to stop and pray, or dance or sing along to a favourite tune, or share moments with special people, 'happy hormones' flood your system, keeping you healthy. For this, you need to first accept that happiness is something that is generated from within, and it comes with time and practice. Happiness, at its core, is about discovering meaning, and counting your blessings, not your woes. Happiness grows in nurturing relationships. All kinds of intentional relational activities — practices in which people actively choose to reach out and engage with and serve others — can offer a promising route to lasting happiness. Happiness then is simply about saying a heartfelt 'yes' to all of life; to more positive emotions, to more engagement, to more meaning and purpose, to more caring relationships.

Guru Retails Bliss, not Happiness

Vithal C Nadkarni

Martin Seligman had his Eureka moment when his five-year-old daughter accused him of being a grouch. He had just been elected president of the American Psychological Association and had criticized the child for being whiny, when she reminded the psychologist, renowned for his research on depression, not to forget how hard she had worked to stop whining. If she could stop whining, the child reasoned, why couldn't her father stop being grumpy? That's when Seligman realized that he, 'a pessimist and a depressive of high critical intelligence', badly needed a 180-degree change of direction.

Positive psychology was born out of his new mission statement: to find out what makes life worth living as opposed to delving into what seemed to make it worthless. The difference was akin to that between a half-full and half-empty glass: one focuses on 'plus' states with the same earnestness that the other brings to the study of 'minus' states or negative emotions.

Traditional psychotherapy thus aims at converting acute human misery into bearable suffering while positive psychology promises to turn mild pleasure into a profound state of well-being, what the Czech writer Milan Kundera called 'the unbearable lightness of being'. Echoing an insight of eastern masters, positive psychologists warn, however, that you should not confuse this state with the garden variety of happiness that comes from, say, a sumptuous meal or climactic coitus. Instead, you need to separate 'doing good' (*sukarma*) that leads to lasting happiness from 'feeling good' which inevitably leads to a hunger or thirst (*trishna*) for more pleasure.

What positive psychology calls the 'hedonic treadmill' could, therefore, be viewed as being equivalent to eastern tradition's endless rounds of *Samsara*. But there are radical differences too: unlike western purveyors of happiness with their pills and potions, eastern spiritual masters never try to make you 'happy'. For that would only condition you to a biological hit or 'fix', with all its attendant downside dangers. Moreover, the aspects that positive psychology emphasizes as worth cultivating — optimism, cheerfulness, gratitude, hope and spirituality — appear to be secondary add-ons of the existential bliss (*ananda*) flowing from liberation (*moksha*). Eastern tradition considers the latter to be life's ultimate goal. The realization of your own essential blissfulness (*sat-chit-ananda*) is, therefore, by definition a unitary state of incomparable fullness that lies beyond the dogmas and divides of opposites.

Critics of irrational exuberance also affirm that unlike happiness, bliss is not a station or a destination. They warn that we shouldn't make the mistake of thinking that we can 'own' happiness just because it happens to be a noun. Happiness is a place to visit, not a place to live. Nor is equipoise (*samatvam*), eastern wisdom's prescription to attain bliss, the same as the euphoria obtained by ebb and flow of the brain's feel-good chemicals. Potential disciples seeking spiritual wisdom of the East should heed a statutory health warning: The guru, who tends to speak in logic-defying koans, is a retailer of bliss, not happiness. Failure to make that distinction could lead the aspirant to crushing disappointment by missing out on both happiness and bliss. Positive psychology would also do well to take on board the millennial insights of eastern wisdom and Oriental masters on their part need to share their techniques of attaining bliss and ecstasy for the benefit of humanity at large.

Affluence cannot Bring Lasting Happiness

Satyendra Garg

The other day I came across an interesting report that despite earning lots of money people in affluent countries are insecure and depressed. Oliver James, a psychologist, during his research found that two-thirds of Britons believed that they cannot afford to buy everything they really need. Though the average income of a British citizen is nearly £23,000 per year, about 50 per cent of people who earned more than £35,000 and about 40 per cent of those who earned more than £50,000 per year felt that they did not have enough money to buy things they need. The psychologist went on to say that this perception promoted selfishness and left people feeling bored, empty and lonely.

The article reminded me of the deep insight enshrined in our scriptures. In Srimad Bhagavatam we come across Yayati who was ruler of a large kingdom with all material resources at his command. He married Devyani, daughter of a renowned sage, Sukracharya. According to legend he was cursed for his infidelity and was made prematurely old and infirm. When he begged for forgiveness, he was told that if somebody willingly exchanged his youth with his old age he could regain his youth. When four of his sons declined to exchange their youth for their father's old age the fifth and youngest son who was aware of the inadequacy and futility of sense enjoyment obliged Yayati and agreed to his request. Youthful once again, Yayati continued his sense enjoyment spree for one thousand years. Still unsatisfied, he craved for more. Fortunately for him wisdom dawned on him and he realized that if sensual enjoyment which he had continued for thousand years could not satisfy him, how was it possible that this will be able to satisfy him in future.

On reflection he realized the futility of material and sensual desires and he made up his mind to leave his kingdom and abjure sense enjoyments. He told his wife Devyani that even if one got all the material wealth of the world — food grains, gold and precious metals, and cattle — this will not satisfy the greed of even one single person who is driven by desire for sensual cravings. In modern parlance it could include money, electronic gadgets, land, shares and all other desirable things. So if the researcher finds that despite having £50,000 as annual income and having all modern gadgets, people are not satisfied and they feel they need more money, it is true that even if one is given the entire wealth of the world one will not be satisfied. Yayati goes on to explain as to why this happens. He says that with every additional sense enjoyment the desire for the same becomes more. The more you enjoy, the cravings become more. For the same level of satisfaction, you need more sense indulgence and because one gets satisfaction from every indulgence, one indulges more. And the vicious cycle goes on. Yayati quotes the example of fire and ghee. He says that with every additional pouring of clarified butter in the form of sense enjoyment the fire of sensual desire grows fiercer and fiercer. By indulgence one can never quench the thirst of sensual urge. Only if one realizes this and gives up this insatiable sense craving, can one achieve that inner satisfaction which leads to bliss and eternal happiness.

The Parable of the Blissful Madman

Jahanavi Shandilya

The Nobel prize-winning mathematician John Nash has a long history of schizophrenia, a mental condition in which the afflicted person creates a delusion of alternative reality. Schizophrenics do this to make so-called normal life bearable for themselves. Very often, those suffering from schizophrenia are creative geniuses. Apart from Nash the long list includes musician Ludwig van Beethoven, painter Vincent Van Gogh, ballet dancer Vaclav Nijinsky and many others.

The life and works of gifted artists and creative geniuses show that their expanded consciousness is completely unconfined, giving rise to extraordinary potential beyond the reach of the average person. There is a tendency in the human psyche to reach for higher forms of consciousness. Access to this state is evident — though temporary — in both schizophrenics and individuals who get inspired by sudden insight. Psychiatry has found no cure so far for schizophrenia and perhaps there is no cure. For, on a deeper level, it could be said of all of us that we are indeed schizophrenics in that the 'normal' lives we lead and believe in, including getting a job, earning a livelihood, raising a family is, when seen from the plane of the spiritually enlightened, nothing but a carefully fabricated illusion very much like what the schizophrenics construct for themselves.

So how do we break out of our delusions? Not necessarily by renouncing the world and all its illusory joys and sorrows, its fictive triumphs and tragedies, but by recognizing the delusional nature of this world. When we lose ourselves in meditation or in the exaltation that great music or art can create, the delusional world with its myriad anxieties and griefs seems to fall away from us and we feel a sense of untrammelled freedom. Nijinsky wrote in his diaries that he was God. This scandalized the pious Christian establishment of his time that considered such utterances as blasphemous. However, what Nijinsky had really done was to achieve, through the discipline of dance, spiritual liberation that revealed the transcendence within.

Nijinsky's story finds a parallel with that of the sage's response to a person who had come to see him for spiritual guidance pleading that his everyday worries, cares, and daily search for meaning in life was driving him 'mad'. The sage heard him out and said, "I do not know if I can cure you of your madness, but right now you are an unhappy madman and I can transform you into a blissful madman."

It should be noted, however, that such spiritual prescriptions are not like over-the-counter drugs that can be bought and sold at will. True spiritual sages never offer a panacea for universal happiness — as distinct from individual bliss — because they know that such a thing is axiomatically impossible. It is only the individual seeker after enlightenment who can hope to ascend the spiritual escalator to an other-worldly joy. 'Unhappy madness' — of which schizophrenia is a severe form — is suffered by all of us who feel the constant pressures of the everyday material world. Blissful madness was what Nijinsky evinced or what the devotional Baul singers experience as do the whirling dervishes who lose themselves in a frenzy of spiritual rapture.

Perhaps that is why the form of madness we call schizophrenia or the more general form of madness called mortal existence cannot be 'cured' but it can be transformed into the inspired, ecstatic madness of spiritual awakening. The other side of madness is not so-called normalcy; it is the beatific insanity of bliss.

Gross National Happiness Indicates True State

Amitava Basu

When happiness is measured in terms of gross national product, it implies value of final goods and services produced in a country within a particular year. Happiness, however, has many dimensions. It is not confined to only income and wealth. For example, a rich businessman may be less happy and grumble more than a content farmer who has a lower standard of living as compared to the businessman. It is discontent or emptiness that the rich man experiences, which constitutes unhappiness. Happiness does not automatically flow from economic prosperity.

People are happy in a society where everyone is safe, where everyone has a decent livelihood, and where everyone has access to education and health care. It is a society where there is less pollution, where there is respect for environment, where inequalities are minimal, and where culture thrives. In a happy society people enjoy freedom, there is no oppression and art, music, dance and drama flourish. It is a caring society — caring for the past and the future, caring for those who need protection. In simple terms, it is a more equal and compassionate society.

To establish such a happiness generating society, policies are needed to link economic progress to human happiness. This requires improvement in socio-economic conditions and satisfaction of basic needs. But growing income and provision of better social services are not sufficient. These need to be supplemented with appropriate employment opportunities, social security and adequate leisure time. A happy society is not fatalistic but is built on hopes and aspirations. The burst of consumer-driven economic growth and consequent explosion of affluence in industrialized societies has had an adverse impact on spiritual advancement. In pursuit of economic prosperity, many societies have lost their spirituality and compromised their environment.

Taking lessons from these experiences, Bhutan, the small and beautiful Buddhist kingdom in the Himalayas, has adopted a different approach for people's welfare. King Jigme Singye Wangchuk espoused the concept of gross national happiness. It calls for careful balance between creation of material wealth and spiritual, cultural and social needs. It recognizes that all efforts should seek to contribute to both material and spiritual well-being of people. The constituents of gross national happiness are not only limited to the flow of money but include access to health care, free time with family, conservation of natural resources and other non-economic factors.

Articulation of happiness as goal of human life has strong roots in Bhutan's Buddhist traditions. It speaks of avoiding dissatisfaction through adequate provision of four basic necessities — food, shelter, clothing and medicine. However, it holds that meeting this hierarchy of wants is only the first step towards abatement of human suffering, which ultimately depends on cultivating a sense of detachment and spiritual fulfilment. The philosophy enshrined in the concept of gross national happiness aims to promote happiness through careful balancing of spiritual, emotional and cultural needs on the one hand and material well-being on the other.

Enjoy to the Hilt the Joy of Being

Swami Kriyananda

A life without joy is not really life; it is death. Jesus said, "Let the dead bury their dead" (Matthew 8:22). He was referring not to corpses getting up and burying other corpses, but to people who walk around, apparently living, but with no life in their hearts, no enthusiasm, no inner happiness. Develop the capacity to feel the symphony of life coursing through the veins of the trees, singing and laughing with the children as they play, scudding with the clouds through the sky. This is life! True happiness has nothing to do with whether one has all the things that money can buy. It can be ours only to the extent that we have life within.

In western thought, we find constantly the emphasis on doing. In the East, being is emphasized. Immanuel Kant said that we should seek happiness for others, not for ourselves. But the sages of India would say that Kant was putting the cart before the horse. For, granting that happiness is man's greatest gift to man, how is it possible to give it if one doesn't first have it oneself ? Can you give away money that isn't yours to give? Will it make people happy to be given only things? Things are not happiness! Often they create conditions that prevent one from happiness. Happiness can be 'caught' only from people who first have it themselves.

George Bernard Shaw was once at a party, sitting by himself on the outskirts of the festivity. The hostess came over and asked him, "Aren't you enjoying yourself?" Shaw replied, "That's all I am enjoying!" The truth is, this is all you can enjoy: yourself. All outer enjoyments are but reflections of the enjoyment you have in yourself.

God is the God of the eternal NOW. To have life means to have this joyful awareness this very moment. Not after we've paid our income tax, or completed the instalments on our new car. To live truly this moment, you must not live for the moment. Moments change; the eternal Now remains constant. This Now is the centre of the wheel around which all outward circumstances revolve. You might say that the difference between saints, who constantly react with joy and wonder to the universe around them, and the average person is that saints truly have life. By contrast the average man is dead. Only the spiritual man is wholly alive, living constantly in the present tense, every atom of his being vibrant with vitality. I have never seen a spiritual person who did not have joy.

Joy, surely, is the greatest hallmark of spirituality. Joy wells up from the depths of a vibrant, inner calmness. When they laugh, we feel like hugging the very air with delight! This world is like a symphony, and God is the great conductor bringing music out of all things. In all things God has assumed different roles. Through sunlight He is saying, "I am power." Through wind He is saying, "I am free!" Through man He is saying, "I am wise. I feel deeply." Through dogs He is saying, "Oh, how playful I am! How wonderful is it to play!" And through birds He is singing, "Oh, what melody there is in my heart!"

When Bliss Alone Exists, can there be Sorrow?

Swami Chidananda

The all-pervading reality that is the centre of your being is experienced as pure bliss. This experience is non-dual, for no second factor exists. If Brahman is bliss and Brahman alone exists; nothing else exists. If only bliss exists, there can be no sorrow. Then why is it that psychiatrists thrive? Why do people commit suicide? Why do we need to send letters of condolence? Where does sorrow come from when Brahman, as Bliss, is all-pervasive? Should not everything be filled with the light of wisdom, instead of the gloom of ignorance? We speak of the guru as one who removes darkness. Where is darkness when everything is filled with light that comes from within you?

May be this is something non-dualists say. But most Christians, Muslims, Jews and many Hindus are not *advaitavadis*, yet they do believe in a universal God. "The Kingdom of Heaven is within. The Light of Allah shines in man." So even from a dualistic point of view, when the presence of God is within, and He is bliss, how can one have sorrow?

It's a paradox. Perhaps we are not perturbed by the contradiction because we are too busy satisfying our senses, fulfilling our desires, seeking sensations, getting enmeshed in names and forms and their changeful play. To resolve this paradox, there must be clarity within.

Several planes of consciousness coexist. We need concern ourselves with only two of them. When you are present-minded, then you are conscious that "I am in Uttarakhand, in *Muni-ki-reti*, on the banks of the Ganga, in Sivananda Ashram, in the Samadhi Hall, early morning, in the spiritual presence of Gurudev." But if you imagine that you are in America or Canada, then at the same time you are not here. On the mental plane if you have switched channels, then you are only perceiving and experiencing whatever is there, and other channels do not exist. Your body is sitting here, but you are not here. So it is possible for layers of consciousness to coexist simultaneously in one and the same time-space frame, in this mental consciousness, active in the waking state.

Also present is your true consciousness, your true plane. You are pure, bereft of this *samsara*. Cast off the sleep of delusion. You are beyond this perceived play, this perceived *drishya* or appearance, this *jagat jal* or world illusion of name and form. You are beyond this *samsaramaya* in your other plane of consciousness, the plane of your nija *svarupa*, your eternal, real identity. So, seemingly there is a contradiction, but there is no contradiction. Because the bliss of Brahmn is never experienced. That plane is never active. But a strange delusion is there, a hallucination, thinking: "Oh, yes, I know, I am Brahman beyond *maya*." Being in *maya*, one says, "I am Brahman beyond *maya*."

We sometimes imagine we are in spiritual consciousness, whereas this is only an idea in the mind. It is not the true spiritual plane of consciousness. Out of 1,00,000 *sadhakas*, 99,999 are living a spiritual life outwardly, but, in fact, their entire life is lived only upon the mental plane, only upon the psychological plane of consciousness. Very rarely does one rise above the psychological plane of consciousness, because to do so requires immense, intense alertness. And this can only come with hard spiritual practice.

Decipher the Formula of Happiness

Kiran Bedi

I prefer reading inspirational writings of people who have lived predominantly selfless lives — people who gave a great deal of themselves to society; who had the option to live comfortably yet chose discomfort (as some would perceive it) for larger good. What makes selfless people so different from the rest of us? One wonders, does it matter if you are rich or poor, educated or illiterate, man or woman? Are selfless people sad or happy people? What is their source of sustained strength? What is their state of mind? Where did their training come from? Are they born with the propensity to act selflessly or did they learn it by trial and error?

All persons whom we tend to admire and want to see and be with, are those whom we have known to remain happy, naturally. Nothing seems to disturb them. They are truly happy within and without. They are not dependent on material acquisitions, nor do they depend on other people to come and make them happy. On the contrary, people seek them out. It could be happiness as they believe it to be...

As I have understood — from reading what these inspirational persons write — happiness is not external. It is truly internal. It is not something they buy or borrow. Nor is it fleeting. It is in their own state of 'minding' which they choose to remain in. And for that state of mind to be integral to them, they gradually schooled, graduated, and mastered the art in such a way that it became 'them'. Even after mastering they remain aware of their learning in such a way that happiness becomes a part of their 'self'. They 'become joy' and 'joy becomes them'.

We, too, can learn from them and begin in small ways to follow the path of living in happiness. It has been said that the longest journey begins with the first step. Happiness, too, is a constant journey of the mind, a journey that we choose to undertake and then stay on. Each moment the mind journeys it will constantly decide to remain on course — first by conscious awareness, then by habit. The mind stays alert on what impacts inner joy and how it constantly rejuvenates itself by self-watch. Having been a sportsperson I am aware that a holiday of one day practice takes one back by three days. So is it with mindfulness. We in our daily lives encounter many (negative) stress-giving situations for which we are not always responsible. There are several kinds of reactions such a situation can evoke: Become unhappy, get angry, fret, frown, become moody, curse and blame others, or nurse retaliation and negative emotions. Or does the mind tell us to do whatever one can do and move on? And even if it warns us, do we listen to it and let it direct our subsequent responses?

Just as a well-tended garden cannot be so without a caring gardener, so, too, a happy human being has a well-tended mind — a mind which constantly self-cares and self-generates joy. It is independent and self-dependent. It gives and reaches out whenever needed, without any declarations. It remains grateful for anything it receives without seeking. And gives away without any asking. It is always there and yet is elsewhere. Empty, yet full

Look for Happiness in the Right Places

B Vichar Vishnu Maharaj

All living beings are full of happiness. Our daily routine, rituals and activities are all directed towards achieving happiness. We might be working with different goals but the ultimate aim is to remain happy. People search for happiness in various spheres of life. Those unable to find happiness in their self or others look outward for extra adventure. What is happiness? Happiness could be defined in many ways. Simply put, happiness is a feeling which imparts pleasure in us. This pleasure is derived either by meeting a friend, or fulfilling a long cherished dream, for instance. Money can help us fulfil our dreams — we can move out, we can buy, we can please others. Happiness is also perceived as what your disposable income can buy. So the struggle continues for that extra sum. No doubt, if you have enough money to lead a comfortable and healthy life, have lot of friends, and enjoy luxuries, you might feel happy. However, even the richest are sometimes unhappy. The learned, too, are not always happy.

Krishna relates in the *Bhagavad Gita* that all living beings are made up of soul, gross body and subtle body. Soul is the master of the body and is composed of *sat-chit-ananda* or everlasting happiness. Though we are made up of happiness, still we look for happiness in external objects. Happiness is a state of mind. So why are we looking for happiness outside? That is because we lack knowledge about ourselves. We study to become successful so that we become happy. While pursuing that goal we forget to attain knowledge of self — we failed to learn about ourselves, to learn where to find that happiness for which we had invested a number of years of our lives.

The basic problem lies with our approach. We are looking for happiness at wrong places. If we approach an ironsmith in search of gold, will we get gold? Similarly, looking for happiness and asking for happiness from beings and objects cannot give happiness. All living beings are full of happiness but are unable to distribute that happiness. To attain happiness we need to approach the one which is treasure of happiness and that is only one, the Absolute Personality of Godhead.

Limited beings tend to remain unhappy as desires are unfulfilled. One may see family disputes when family members pursue different goals. If we draw a number of circles with a common epicentre, they will never intersect. However, if we draw number of circles with different epicentres, they are bound to intersect. This happens when we begin pursuing different goals. Our desires clash. The root cause of problems lies in the sphere of their desire. If one begins to work for the happiness of all and for the pleasure of others, it is going to please all. If everybody is pleased, the very atmosphere is cheerful. Once one begins giving, others will reciprocate. Newton's law of equal and opposite reaction works here as well. In the *Bhagavad Gita,* Krishna confirms that He will reciprocate when He tells Arjuna, "Those who always worship Me with exclusive devotion, meditating on My transcendental form — to them I carry what they lack, and I preserve what they have." What other assurance does one need?

Mathematical Equation for Eternal Happiness

KS Iyer

The definition of happiness varies from person to person. It varies even from one stage of life to another. Is it possible to arrive at a formula that conforms to everyone's definition of happiness? MK Gandhi found an answer to this question in the first verse of the Isha Upanishad that said, "Renounce and enjoy." This was his reply to a western journalist who challenged him to reveal the secret of his happiness in just three words.

When we express this secret in mathematical terms, the connection between renunciation and happiness becomes clear: $H = R/N$ — where H stands for happiness/contentment, R for resources at your command and N for your needs. As the quantum of your needs starts decreasing the 'H' quotient keeps increasing. If you can bring down the 'N' factor to zero, 'H' reaches infinity. Such a feat is almost impossible for the average person. Also, there is a danger of misinterpreting the concept of renunciation. It is not the gloominess of self-denial but the extinguishing of the candle because dawn has arrived. It is a highly evolved mind that understands that it is better to need less than to want and have more.

Most live out their lives assuming that existing resources are insufficient to fulfil our needs. This economic thought process leads to 'scarcity' and so there arises conflict, each individual or a group fighting for himself or itself.

The Isha Upanishad invocation contradicts all that. Social Darwinism is based on the economics of materialism. But spiritual economics begins not from the assumed scarcity of matter but from the verifiable infinity of contentment.

This argument sounds logical and convincing, but how practical is it? We live in a flat world where other people's affluence sets standards for us. We need to break the mould of consumerist thinking. That the materialistic West is increasingly turning to the spiritual East for inspiration is an eye-opener. When Gandhi used ahimsa or non-violence to overcome the British dominion, the idea was dismissed by many as being impractical. But ahimsa did win.

In our pursuit of happiness we must be wrong somewhere; for happiness seems to have become a rare commodity. Those seeking happiness through material acquisitions find their quest is futile. Even though we tire ourselves in search of happiness it is doubtful if we would recognize it if we did find it. Do we really know what makes us happy? A successful person by society's standards is not necessarily a happy person. Because happiness has nothing to do with possessions, environment or even physical health. Happiness comes from a source that is independent of all these. Genuine happiness is a state of contentment that comes with peace of mind and a sense of well-being regardless of outward circumstances.

You will find happiness when you stop comparing your life and possessions with other people's. There will always be bigger houses, better and more expensive than the one we have. Accept the fact that there are some things in life that you can't change. God's blessings come to us in three forms — pleasure, joy and happiness. Pleasure comes from satisfying our physical senses, joy comes from association with others but happiness results from a fulfilling relationship with God. Everything comes from God and returns to God. And God has provided enough for everyone's need but not for everyone's greed.

Learn where to Look for Happiness

Swami Sukhabodhananda

The morning sun was accompanied by a cool breeze. The rain overnight had soaked the earth. Crimson rays of the rising sun played on patches of water to create a riot of colours on the ground. Chirping birds sang in chorus. Butterflies flitted about in step with the song of the birds. It was a mix of wonderful sights and sounds. A bird invited me to its world of melody.

Why is love a stranger in our lives? Where is the urge to overcome separation in love? When physically apart, we can feel the separation — we pine for the loved one who is far away. At the spiritual level, however, physicalities do not matter. At this level, you do not have to strive to become One, for you are One. The urge to become One at the physical level alone is a great source of unhappiness.

A young man once asked me, "Is it possible to be happy in this competitive world? It appears that we succeed only when we cheat others. Can one really build a happy life on a foundation of distrust?" An Indian maxim goes like this: "However hard you search in the mouth of a crow, you will not find any teeth there." Many of us search for happiness where it does not exist. The Bible says, "The Kingdom of heaven is within you." The *Gita* says, 'Happiness is within'. But we search for happiness not within ourselves but outside. We get lost in the details and forget the essence... that lies in ourselves.

Most of us are busy with the trivialities of life and in the process miss the essential. We are unhappy in life because we are victims of our expectations. We have to learn the art of side-stepping our expectations. You might ask, "How can we live without expectations?"

My question is: "Have expectations made our life easier or more difficult?" We suffer on account of expectations. We do not trust our intelligence; but we trust our expectations. Have expectations, but let not your happiness depend on them. Operate from love, not expectations. Love provides caring energy. This energy will make you effective and happy.

There was a Zen master. He was frail but had a powerful presence. He could push huge boulders effortlessly. Someone asked him, "What is the secret of your strength? Where does it come from?"

The Zen master replied, "Before pushing a boulder, I communicate with it, request its permission and support in my effort. And then the boulder gets moved miraculously...." Power comes from the mystery of love, not from our expectation of how others should behave.

A carpenter from China created a unique piece of furniture. It was a piece of art, and was liked by many. When asked how he made it, the carpenter replied, "Before cutting a tree in the forest, I talk to it and take its permission, intuitively understanding which tree would submit to being felled. The furniture made out of such a tree will always be a piece of art."

Love has power, the power to create. It is this power we should learn to draw from. If our expectations emerge from love, we become masters of our expectations. Otherwise we are slaves to them. Misery is not a product of a cut-throat world; it is the result of expectations from a world bereft of love.

Vedantic Life of Action, Peace & Happiness

Swamy Parthasarathy

Living is an art, a skill, a technique. Few understand it to be so; you need to learn and practise the technique as you would be playing a musical instrument or flying an aircraft. The process of learning how to live is not taught in school or university. People go through a mechanical way of living merely following a routine of their predecessors. They lack this fundamental knowledge of living and become victims of stress and strain.

Everywhere people have lost pleasure in action. They try to find peace and happiness by abstaining from action. Hence, everyone looks forward to weekends and vacations or seek premature retirement. If you cannot find peace and happiness in action you can never find it through abstinence.

There are two distinct classes of people. One is active, productive and prosperous. The western world seems to fit this category. But by their own admission they have lost peace of mind. The other class of people is relatively peaceful and happy but without much action. Since they lack action, they are not productive and prosperous. Some eastern countries face this problem. Thus there is action without peace on one side and peace without action on the other. Is it possible to combine dynamic action with mental peace?

Vedanta provides the answer. The few who have imbibed the knowledge of Vedanta, learnt and practised the technique of living, live a dynamic life of action while enjoying perfect peace and happiness within. Vedanta helps you evolve to greater heights in your own spiritual path. It provides you with knowledge and guidance to reach the ultimate in human perfection. The goal of Self-realization ploughs through human ignorance and delusion to discover the pristine glory of one's supreme Self. Vedanta is systematic knowledge that explains the meaning and purpose of your existence in the world. A knowledge that is founded on its own authority. It trains you to think for yourself. To analyse, investigate and realize the quintessence of life. Not to submit yourself to blind faith, superstitious belief or mechanical ritual. Ultimately, it leads you to spiritual enlightenment.

The knowledge of the unknown can be gained only through the use of known factors. Therefore, to unravel the mystery of God you need to use the world of objects and beings known to you. Start with the study of the world, the individual and the relationship between them. It is not the world that bothers you but your relationship with it. You need to learn the principles of right living. Change the character of your action from selfishness to selfless service. Mend the quality of your emotion from preferential attachment to universal love. Raise your knowledge from the mundane to the supreme Self within.

Vedanta further explains the composition of a human being. The five layers of human personality enveloping the inner Self. The three states of conditioned-consciousness known as waking, dreaming and deep sleep. Every individual experiences the cycle of these states. None realizes pure Consciousness, Core of one's being. Vedanta directs you to discover the Core, the supreme Self within. A Self-realized person is one with God. He revels in absolute peace and bliss. Becomes a beacon for the rest of the world to follow and steer their lives towards evolution.

The Way to Achieve Lasting Happiness

Swami Tejomayananda

appiness is of three kinds: *Sattvika, rajasika* and *tamasika*. The *Gita* says *sattvika* happiness is that which initially appears to be akin to poison but ultimately it is like nectar. If we are used to late nights, then getting up early morning to study or exercise is very difficult, But if we do wake up early and do such activities regularly, it results in long-lasting happiness.

Sattvika happiness is born out of grace, blessings and Self-knowledge. Generally our mind is extrovert. We know well the joy of sense pleasure, but we do not know the joy which is possible in a mind that is pure, contemplative, and in meditation. If we get a taste of such happiness we will leave *rajasika* and *tamasika* joys. The glamour and charm of sense pleasures no longer hold any attraction. When the source of happiness is discovered in our hearts, we will no more depend on the world to derive happiness. Such happiness is seen in the life of men like Ramakrishna Paramhansa, Ramana Maharshi, Swami Chinmayananda and others. Despite their physical ailments they remained ever blissful. But for this one has to live a life of discipline with regular spiritual practice and study of the scriptures, and meditation. These seem difficult but result in happiness.

The *Gita* says *rajasika* happiness is that which arises out of contact between the sense organs and sense objects. It initially is like nectar but results in sorrow like poison. Such happiness depends on external factors like availability of the object, and mood for enjoyment. *Rajasika* joy leads to greed, a glimpse of it to dissatisfaction, more of it to indulgence, repetition, repetition to addiction, loss of it to pain and so on. No pain arises from realizing the source of happiness within. None complains of too much happiness or boredom with external bliss. But one does get sick of sense pleasures and the law of diminishing returns comes into play. Hence, even if there may be initial joy, *rajasika* happiness is momentary, enslaving and problematic.

The *Gita* says *tamasika* happiness is that which deludes a person in the beginning and end and arises out of laziness and forgetfulness. The joy of sleep is *tamasika* but it is vital for us to get refreshed and rejuvenated. But the joy referred to here is the joy of a person who sleeps all the time. One is physical sleep, and the other is sleep of ignorance from which people do not wish to be awakened. They declare that 'ignorance is bliss' and wish to remain in it. One experiences the joy of being lazy and postponing work.

One remembers duties but does not do them. Some do not even remember them. Some are quite proud of forgetting them and give it as a seemingly valid excuse for not doing the task. Some revel in the joy of drinking, smoking, getting stoned, gambling and so on. These habits completely delude one's mind and such a person cannot achieve anything high or noble. In fact, the person suffers all the time, but deludes himself into thinking that he is enjoying life. There is no peace, no inner satisfaction, and no sense of achievement or success.

Sattvika happiness appears difficult initially, but results in lasting happiness and liberates like nectar. *Rajasika* happiness is like poison and *tamasika* happiness deludes one, stops all progress. One with a *sattvika* vision, understanding and fortitude surely gets *sattvika* happiness.

Joy is your Very Nature, Make it Sustainable

Sadhguru

What is joy about? Joy is definitively not about anything, because joy is not something that you do; joy is something that you become. If you do not disturb the basic process of life within you, joy is a natural outcome. Joy is not an achievement, joy is your original state.

In yoga, we are looking at a human being as a strata of five bodies. In the original terminology, we say *Annamaya, Manomaya, Pranamaya, Vignanamaya* and *Anandamaya Koshas* — physical, mental, energy, etheric and joy or bliss bodies. Bliss body is not the appropriate word. The deepest core of you is not joy. But it is the non-physical. As that which is non-physical can neither be defined nor described, we are referring to it from the context of our experience. When we are in touch with this non-physical dimension our experience is blissful and thus the term bliss body.

Most do not know joy because their physical, mental and energy bodies are not in alignment. The core of you is joy, over that there are four layers. If they are properly aligned, an overwhelming expression of joyfulness will naturally happen. People may achieve this state in different ways, but it doesn't last. Now we are looking at the technology of keeping these three bodies constantly aligned so that joyfulness is not an accidental happening; joyfulness becomes a normal condition, a natural way of living for you. A sustainable state.

In yoga, Brahmanand means that Creation is joy. What you see as the physical, mental, or physical energies is just the surface; the deeper core, the source of creation, is joyfulness. If the Creator is joyful, sitting somewhere in heaven — what is the point? The Creator or what you refer to as the source of creation is not sitting somewhere else. If you look at your own body, from the moment of birth to now, how much it has grown, and this growth did not happen because of any external stretching, this happened from within; the source of creation is constantly in function.

The source of Creation is within you right now. That is joyfulness. Once this fundamental force of Creation finds expression in your life and you allow it to move out, joyful is the only way you can be. If you are not entangled with the modifications of your mind, joyfulness is a natural way. Outside situations can cause physical pain; suffering and misery are always created in the mind. When you were a child, you were joyful by nature. You did not need much to be joyful. Somebody had to make you miserable, that was your condition. But today, somebody has to make you joyful. People are hoping that someday, somebody will come and make them joyful. If you depend on the outside to bring joy to you, only by accident you will be joyful, not by intent. Outside situations never happen 100 per cent the way you want it. Not one person in this world is exactly the way you want them to be. So when this is the reality, at least this one person — you — must be the way you want to be.

If you are the way you want yourself to be, the natural choice is joy. What we are talking about as Inner Engineering or inner sciences is not seeing joy as something that you have to attain, but seeing joy as the very basis of your life. If you get in tune with your own basic existence, joyful is the only way you will be.

Joy is Short-lived, Bliss is Eternal

Ashutoshji Maharaj

Why is it said that perfect beings dwell in the state of *ananda* or bliss and not that of *sukha* or joy? Once there was an affluent merchant. He owned many palatial houses and factories. One of his mansions suddenly caught fire. The merchant was devastated. Seeing his grief, his servant consoled him, saying, "Why do you worry? Don't you remember that only few days ago your son finalized a sale deed?" Now the merchant was filled with joy. He even increased the servant's salary. After a while, the merchant's son came home, looking crestfallen. His father said, "It is good you sold that house; otherwise, we would have faced a great loss today."

The son replied, "Father, I fixed a deal for selling that house, but the payment is yet to be received. And now the buyer is refusing to make the payment." As soon as the merchant heard these words his joy disappeared. He was now sad.

Joy is short-lived, because it relies on external circumstances. Bliss is eternal for it comes from within. Its source is God, the eternal *sat-chit-ananda*. When a seeker finds God within he is able to attain the supreme state of bliss.

One day, Mehta Kalu, father of Guru Nanak Dev, said, "Nanak, now you have stepped into your youth. You should start some business. Go, buy some goods at reasonable price from another village, come back and sell them a bit dearly here." Mehta Kalu handed over some cash to his son and Nanak set off. In a little while he came across a congregation of saints. They were singing the glory of God and were dancing, fully absorbed in God's ecstasy. This attracted Nanak who listened to their spiritual discourses and enjoyed the melody of the devotional songs sung by them. Intoxicated by blissful devotion, Nanak spent all the money he had in buying food for those saints. When he returned home empty-handed,

Mehta Kalu inquired, "What happened? Did you make some deal on the way itself ?"

Nanak answered in an inebriated tone, still absorbed in the bliss of Lord, "Yes, father, the deal was fixed on the way. And that too the purely honest and real one!" Thereafter, Nanak recounted what he had experienced to his father. Mehta Kalu flew into a temper. Nanak, however, remained calm, immersed as he was in the blissful pool of devotion. Mehta Kalu, influenced by worldly gains and losses, swung between joy and dejection. However, Nanak dwelt in the spiritual realm. He was always absorbed in bliss-consciousness that prevailed over the bounds of the influence of worldly gains and losses.

The one who is established in soul-consciousness is always immersed in the ecstatic bliss of the Lord's name. He is never haunted by feelings of despair and dejection. However, the prerequisite for attaining such a blissful state is Brahmn Gyan — the revelation and manifestation of the effulgent form of the Lord in the innermost realms of heart. When you have a glimpse of the divine, ever effulgent form of Lord, when you merge in Him, only then can you experience transcendental bliss. Strive to attain the realization of God through a Perfect Master, and elevate yourself from short-lived joy to eternal bliss.

Happiness is Temporary, Bliss is Eternal

Swami Kriyananda

Happiness for most people begins with the thought: "This is how things ought to be!" Suffering comes with the opposite thought: "Things ought not to be as they are". However, we tend to fall into the habit of thinking that we know already how things ought to be or ought not to be. We identify happiness with fixity instead of accepting life's natural flow. We become 'psychological antiques' — wanting nothing moved, nothing changed, nothing even improved. The stability comes to mean permanence. Permanence, however, is something the soul can have only in God.

Happiness is bliss outwardly directed towards the senses and their world of relativity and change. Bliss is eternal, but happiness is man's attempt to project bliss into a fleeting and alien environment. In that projection, he forms attachments to things temporal. Happiness, in its pretence of permanence, becomes simply another counterfeit, like pleasure. People's search for outward stability is often visualized by them as a fixed place on earth, a home of their own. Imagine that place as they often conceive it: a picturesque cottage by the sea, its entrance graced by a rose trellis, its well-manicured lawn bordered by colourful flowers, the garden enlivened by gay song birds. The interior of the cottage is cosily furnished with good books, paintings, furniture. 'Wee Nook' we'll call it; countless 'dream cottages' bear that quaint, if somewhat cloying, name! This is a place for putting down one's roots.

Now, visualize the dream lasting... and lasting... and lasting! No matter how pleasant, might it not last too long? Ten years might already be overdoing it — but eternity? Any happiness you find at Wee Nook would certainly become stale, eventually; your 'fulfilment' might well become more a burden than a joy. Someday you'd surely find yourself crying out in desperation, "Somebody — something:

Please knock me on the head to convince me I'm still alive!" Boredom is a very different condition, certainly, from bliss!

What everyone really wants is bliss. Happiness is a counterfeit: too much of it diffuses one's very concept of bliss. To a mind full of attachments, bliss seems almost a threat. A cottage by the sea is something the ego, at least, can handle without effort. But bliss? Bliss requires total absorption. Few people are ready to be all that happy! They need suffering, to spur them towards ever higher aspiration.

A bird, after 20 years of living in a cage, would be afraid to leave it. Were the cage door opened, the bird would cower at the back, dreading the flight that is perfectly natural for it. Man, at the thought of absorption in bliss, faces two major challenges. First, to his mind, bliss implies a need for exerting high energy. Second, the concept of absolute consciousness seems to him overwhelming.

If you have attained a certain degree of refinement, you would be unwilling to return to living like others who limit their pleasures to the table, their barroom, and the bedroom. Creatures at every stage of evolution cling to what is familiar to them. Familiarity gives them their sense of security. And so, they may meet the call to higher awareness with stout resistance.

The principal challenge bliss presents is the demand that one's ego be abandoned. Human beings define themselves in terms of their bodies. They think of themselves as having a specific age, name, nationality, sex and social position. These do not, however, truly define us at all. In infinite consciousness, not even self-awareness, ultimately, is lost; it is simply transformed. Nothing, in essence, can be either created or destroyed.

Give up Pleasure so you can Know Bliss

B Ballabh Tirtha Maharaj

What we call pleasure or path of pleasure, the scriptures term as Yogakshema. It means that you give your full energy to gain objects of enjoyment, so that you can experience sense gratification. In this way, all your energy is spent in the pursuit of money and objects of enjoyment. After attaining all these things, you attempt to retain them. After earning money, all your energy is spent in trying to preserve it.

Kathopanishad says there are always two options. One is the path for gaining eternal welfare and the other, for obtaining apparent sense-pleasures. Human beings are divided into two categories: Those who adopt the path of eternal welfare (*shreyah*) and who take to sense pleasure (*preyah*). Although something may be pleasing to the material senses, the consequences will be detrimental. If, however, you take the path of *shreyah*, at first it will be unpleasant because you have to restrict and withdraw your senses. You have to be regulated. You cannot do whatever you like. But the fruit, the ultimate result, is ambrosia.

When a young boy learns to drive a vehicle, his immediate desire is to drive on the road. An inexperienced driver may cause havoc on a highway. However, to avoid such mishappenings, a fresher has to pass through various processes to get a licence and for a few months he has to remain a learner-driver. The result eventually is good for all. We have to choose between *shreyah* and *preyah marg*.

Srimad Bhagavatam states that human birth is *Su-durlabham* — 'extremely difficult to get'. One may get human birth after numerous births. Specifically after 80 lakh births in various species. Scriptures confirm that one takes birth as an aquatic animal. How many times? Nine lakh. You will find many people catching fish and killing them. We also, at some time, have been caught and devoured by them. So much suffering is there! We call this 'survival of the fittest'. But even the big fish are not safe in the sea. In this way, we pass through nine lakh lives as aquatic animals. We are also born as trees, mountains and hills, One may argue, 'A hill is inert. How can a living being become lifeless?' A hill is not inert. It grows, but it has an enveloped consciousness. Trees also have some sensation. They have life. Twenty lakh of births we pass this way. So much suffering! There are 11 lakh species of worms. After that we have 10 lakh births as birds. Then 30 lakh births as beasts. Finally come human birth.

What do we require? Unless we get absolute bliss, we cannot be happy. We may satisfy our immediate needs. But you can get absolute bliss by knowing the Supreme. We say that we shall do it in the next birth, but there is no guarantee that in the next birth it will happen.

Most people are running after sensuous, apparent enjoyment. They are not serious about consequences. But those who are wise, who have depth of heart, know that if you adopt the path of pleasure, you will become entangled in this world of temporary things. You will be in bondage.

If, however, you adopt the *shreyah* path, then you will get absolute bliss. Only a wise can differentiate between *shreyah* and *preyah*. If you take to the path of *shreyah*, you can obtain the Supreme, Who is All-bliss. If you adopt the path of pleasure of the senses, it will seem like ambrosia at first, but the consequences will be like poison. You choose.

All Art is Spiritual, Blissful Experience

ML Varadpande

Indian tradition considers all arts to be of divine origin. Art is spiritual in nature and is a blissful way of reaching and staying with God. According to the Shantiparva of *Mahabharta*, Maharishi Jaimini was among the erudite disciples of Vyasa. Literary traditions say that he wrote his own version of the *Mahabharta*. However, except for the Ashvamedha Parva Chapter, the rest is lost. An interview legend is recorded in this work signifying the importance of performing arts as spiritual modes of God-realization over yoga, *dhyana, tapa* and *dana*.

It says, one day Krishna was transfixed by a dancer's dexterity. Delighted, the dancer proclaimed "O ye yogis, see for yourselves that Hari whom you could not realize through meditation and severe penance is before me in person. *Dhyana, tivra-tapa* and fasts pale before dancing, singing and playing of musical instruments which delight God the most."

Bharat Muni in his Natya Shastra states, "The Gods are never so pleased on being worshipped by scents and garlands as they are delighted with the performance of dramas." Theatre evolved through religious rituals. Dialogue hymns or Samvad Suktas of the Rig Veda testify that as rudimentary playlets they formed an integral part of Vedic rituals. In his play Malavikagnimitra poet Kalidasa described dramatic performance as *kratu* or *yajna* itself. Gradually drama got separated from ritual but the tradition of staging plays during *yajna* ceremonies continued.

In temples of Puri, Bhubaneswar and Konark, one can see Natya *mandirs* or halls purported for music and dramatic performance as they were part of temple rituals. Grammarian Patanjali records in his Mahabhashya that musical instruments such as *mridanga, shankha* and *tunava* would be sounded as part of the ritual.

The Rig Veda describes Indra as Nrutu or dancer. Maruts, friends of Indra, were called dancers with golden ornaments. Ashvins, horse-faced physicians of gods, too, were fond of dancing. Sayana refers to dancing gods as *nrutyamano devata*. Shiva is dancer par excellence, Nataraj. Shaivite Karana (dance postures) series are found sculpted in a number of south Indian temples. Cosmic dance of Shiva is described by Acharya Nandikeshvara in his Abhinaya Darpana. He says, "Entire activity going on in the universe is his *angika abhinaya* and whole of literature is his *vachikam*. Celestial bodies such as Chandra and Tara form his *aharya* and he himself is Sattva incarnate." In the Bhagavata Purana Krishna and Balarama are described as two handsome actors. Tradition says that when Krishna danced on the hoods of serpent Kalia, Natavari Nritya or Kathak came into being.

Painting was an exalted form of spiritual art. Chitra Sutra of Vishnudharmottara Purana says that the art of painting, apart from giving dharma and *kama*, liberates human beings from earthly bonds and grants moksha, final liberation. Rasa is the soul of all arts. Vishvanatha in his Sahitya Darpan describes the bliss derived from arts as Brahmaswada *sahodara* or same as experiencing Brahmn. Arts are manifestations of Brahmn. Brahmn is *rasa* and is pure bliss. Bliss-giving Brahmn under the name Rasa is the central principle of all arts. *Rasa* is purely spiritual experience of supreme bliss.

Be both Blissful & Socially Compatible

Sadhguru

You can think about God, liberation, spirituality, but the thought itself can never be spiritual; it is a psychological process. Mind, body and emotion are different dimensions of life. There is nothing right or wrong about them. It all depends on how you use them — but they cannot be spiritual. Spirituality does not belong to the physical realm. It is a dimension beyond the integrated mechanism of body, mind, emotion and physical energy. A human being is just the play of the five elements: water, earth, air, fire and space. But this play is so beautifully constructed that it is complete by itself. Though this and the rest of existence are of the same material, because of its integrity, it looks absolutely individual right now.

Creation is so perfect within itself, you could forget the Creator, and still it would go on. Creation does not need to draw from anything. The problem is, once you realize the perfection of what this is, you will forget God and will lean on something else. If you do not lean on anything else, if you do not need anything from the outside, either a relationship, psychological or emotional help, nothing, you become like the Creator. A piece of creation naturally transforms itself into the Creator itself. If you just want to cross the limitations of your existence, if you just want to enjoy the freedom and bliss of it, all it takes is an intense focus towards any one thing. This is not possible for people who are doing too many things at the same time. If you want to get somewhere, you have to stick to one thing.

There are four dimensions of yoga: *gnana, bhakti, karma* and *kriya*. People who are highly intellectual, who are totally up there, are socially incompatible. Those who are absolutely devoted, they are also socially incompatible. People who are totally in service, they are socially incompatible. Those who are too much on energy, they are also socially incompatible. If these four dimensions are handled in even balance, you can attain the height of experience and yet be socially compatible. If you have to go beyond the barriers of what is considered normal and still be socially compatible, it is important that your body, mind, emotion and energy are evenly cultivated. Only then you can be utterly blissful and still be efficient and capable in everything that you do. Once this is achieved, there is tremendous freedom to create anything that you want around you or within you or anywhere in the world because the very fundamentals of life are in your hands. Suddenly, there is no more limitation of time and space. If this capability has to come, the first thing is to get into ecstatic states, absolutely mindless ecstasy.

Those who are not willing to work to achieve ecstasy choose alcohol or drugs. If people create some sense of freedom chemically or by other external means, you will notice when they don't have that support, they become utterly miserable. If people just escape by chance, if they have not built their own ladder to climb at will, they get psychologically broken.

Enlightenment is beyond logic. There is nothing, so you cannot ruin it. When there is nothing, then everything flows through you. Whatever has to happen in this Existence, it has to flow through you; you become the gateway. If you have the inclination, Existence is within your grasp. You can explore almost everything.

Keep it Simple & you'll be Happy

Dada J P Vaswani

How many gadgets modern technology has blessed us with! Yet, they only seem to add to the stress and tension of our lives. I have seen young men and women walk down parks and green lanes with earphones completely shutting out the world of beauty around them.

Keep it simple! That is the mantra which can help you reduce stress and tension. Possessions and acquisitions may seem marvellous. But after a while, you do not own them, they own you. A Tao story tells us of an artist who was so gifted that his fame spread all over. One day, he painted the picture of a snake. It was so lifelike that viewers seemed to hear it hiss! The artist was so carried away by his own success and the adulation of his fans that he touched up the snake. He made its eyes glow; he outlined the fangs so that they seemed to dart at you! He could not stop; he went on and painted feet on the snake! The expression, 'Painting feet on a snake', a Chinese saying, refers to situations that are needlessly made more complicated by people who do not know when and where to stop.

When our life becomes complicated with power and possessions, we move farther and farther away from the simple joys and pleasures of life. We fail to notice the green grass and the fresh morning flowers. We don't have time to hear birds singing or watch our little ones smiling. We drift away from the state of childlike innocence and simple joy, which is our basic nature. Simplicity is not self-denial. It is a return to those values that matter most in life. It emphasizes spontaneity and intuition. It helps us to rediscover the feeling of wonder and joy that we have lost as adults.

There was a wealthy businessman, who was also a sincere, simple soul. He owned an expensive jet in which he flew about from place to place. They asked him if he enjoyed his private plane. His reply was significant. He said it was certainly very convenient; but he had managed to travel without his own plane earlier; in fact, when he was young and poor, the fact that he couldn't fly did not stop him from being happy.

A famous actress was being interviewed on television. She had made a fortune that year, over a billion dollars. "Does it make you feel good?" she was asked.

"Yes and no," she replied thoughtfully. "Everyone thinks it's marvellous. So many people flock around me. But I really do not know who my true friends are and who are with me only for the money and the glamour. As for my daily life, it has not changed much, except that I work harder now."

A group of young men and women were walking across a shopping mall. They were happy and relaxed; they were talking and laughing merrily. Not a care in the world did they seem to have. There was a young girl among them, who happened to glance at the window of a jewellery store which they passed. On display was a beautiful, brilliant diamond bracelet. How it sparkled and shone! The girl's eyes opened wide. She went close to the window to inspect the price. She could not afford it. She caught up with her friends but she was not the happy, laughing, bubbly girl that she had been five minutes earlier. Her cheerful, buoyant attitude had been replaced by a mood of glum disappointment. This is the worst part about wanting things. Getting them may give you momentary happiness. But not being able to get them often makes you miserable!

Feeling Blissful is only the Beginning

Sadhguru

The moment I say "spirituality", people say, "Yes, I want to be peaceful." If you take a long walk and lie down, you will sleep peacefully. If you eat a good dinner, you will sleep peacefully. You don't need the spiritual process to be peaceful. The longing for peace has essentially come from troubled minds of those who are torturing themselves — for them, peace is a big commodity that they have to seek. If you are not using your mind for self-torture, why would you think of peace? Would you seek exuberance of life or would you seek peace?

You 'rest in peace'. If you want to be peaceful, you must be dead. Now is the time to live. But for those who have lost control over their mental faculty what should have been a miracle has become a misery-manufacturing machine. Even being ecstatic is not a goal by itself. If you are blissful by your own nature, then the important thing is, you are not the issue anymore. If you are an issue yourself, what other issue will you take into your hands? You will not touch anything. When you are no more an issue, then you are willing to plumb the whole of existence to know what it is all about.

Mysticism evolved only in those places where people learnt the technology of being ecstatic by their own nature. For you to experience a little bit of pleasantness within you, if you have to drink, dance, or do something crazy, you will never explore other dimensions of life because keeping yourself pleasant itself is a great challenge and a full-time job. For most, the pursuit of happiness has become the goal of life. Happiness is not something you achieve. It is something that you start with; it is the square one of life. As children, we all started joyfully without any hassle. So, do not understand the spiritual process as one of peace, joy or even bliss. Only if you are blissful, you will truly explore all aspects of life.

There was a time when we believed that whether the tree in our garden bears fruit or not depended on God's will. But we took charge of these things. Now we know if this tree is not bearing fruit what the problem is. We know what to do. So, when you understand that if your Self has not blossomed, it has got nothing to do with anything except that you are not doing the right thing with yourself. Once we understand that, the spiritual process actually begins.

Once you are not an issue, being peaceful, joyful or blissful is not an effort anymore; then naturally you want to know what is behind everything. This is not an induced quest, seeking comes naturally. The spiritual process is not a conscious choice; it is a kind of compulsive behaviour. But unless you handle it consciously, it will not yield. Longing for the boundless is compulsive, but unless you become conscious, it will never work.

If you want to know, experience and handle other dimensions, it is important that you have no rigid structures in your mind. The biggest thing in existence is not a god sitting somewhere. The life process itself contains the creation and the Creator. If you are willing to go beyond the surface substance of what you call yourself, suddenly everything is malleable. Here and There, Now and Then all merge. The individual and the universal are different no more. Unless one experiences the universality of one's nature, human form is wasted. To eat, sleep, reproduce and die, you do not need a human body, intelligence and awareness. Every worm or insect can fulfil that better than a human being.

Many Paths to Bliss

Shri Nimishananda

Sanatana Dharma, which means 'eternal principles of wisdom' can be approached and accessed in three ways: Through the Vedas, through the Upanishads and through the Puranas like Shrimad Bhagavatam and Devi Mahatmyam. The fire rituals or *havans* that we perform today have come to us from the Vedic Age. Despite this, the pure, austere lifestyle of that age is impossible for most of us to practise in this hectic, demanding modern world. The Puranic approach is generally for those of us who are more religious in the traditional sense as it establishes a culture or *sanskar* of rites and ritualistic worship. Though primordial, pure, cosmic consciousness is beyond time and space, it is easier for the average individual to relate to God through divine forms with specific attributes. So, with their own charged consciousness, they invoked this primordial energy to manifest through a form. Mantras came to be revealed in the process. Each mantra has the divine power to invoke a particular deity. Whenever we chant that mantra with faith and devotion, we start vibrating to the frequency of that deity to receive Grace. The 18 major Puranas of Sanatana Dharma describe the qualities, origin, mystical symbolism and power of these deities through vibrations.

In the Upanishadic approach we understand how to recognize and realize divinity in us in relation to the cosmic power. Our sages experimented in subtle inner realms by following a set of principles with complete awareness for long periods until they reached a state of bliss which was automatic and ecstatic. In this enlightened state, they found that they were permanently free of thoughts, desires, negativity, expectations and limitations of all kinds. So, they codified these principles in Upanishads and passed them on to their disciples. In Sanskrit 'Upanishad' means to 'sit close to the *sadguru*', ie, to sit at the lotus feet of the guru as a disciple and imbibe wisdom.

The *sadguru* triggers the notion of Self-enquiry in the disciple, thus activating his innermost core. The disciple's life then follows a path of dynamic motion and evolution within. *Satsangs* are spiritual forums where inner exploration is done with fellow seekers and guidance of the *sadguru*. This is the true *gurukul* where we are inspired to practise Self-enquiry. When the *sadguru* enters our lives energy ignites our awareness invoking divinity, inner faith and stability. So, as we evolve spiritually, our worldly life also becomes free from troubles, problems and worries because we start burning our karmas away. Each day is stable, joyous and fulfilling. The soul's qualities of love, peace, patience, tolerance, compassion, care and share blossom in us, harmoniously integrating spiritual progress and material prosperity. Sanatana Dharma gives us simple, effective and practical formulae to reorient our lives within the framework of *satya, dharma, ahimsa* and *prema* or truth, noble principles, non-violence and unconditional love. By walking in the footsteps of realized sages, we learn how to shed our limitations and live constantly in the blissful core of Self.

A Bliss beyond Words

Vivek Jain

At the core of Jaina ethics lies this realization: "Just as I do not like pain, so does no one else in this world like pain." It is worth recalling the ethical values that follow from this realization today, which is the 2,598th birth anniversary of Vardhamana Mahavira, the 24th Jaina tirthankara. Jainism stands on the foundation of dualism, seeing reality as constituted of two separate and eternal entities: soul (*jiva*) and non-soul (*ajiva*). By nature, each soul is pure, possessing infinite knowledge, bliss and power. But these faculties are restricted by foreign matter — karma — coming in contact with the soul. To be freed from the shackles of karma, one must stop the influx of new karmas while also eliminating acquired ones. It is only then, as the soul passes through progressive stages of spiritual development (*gunasthanas*), that it will ultimately be free of all karma bondages. The process is a complicated one, and can only be undertaken by one who follows the rigorous life of the ascetic.

The life of a true Jaina householder — *asravaka* — is merely a preparation for asceticism. Progress along the path leading even to this level is a laborious one. Religious treatises on the subject prescribe eleven different stages for the path, each one technically called a *pratima* (the word literally means an image, but can be compared to a rung), on each of which the aspirant must achieve perfection before moving on to the next.

The eleven essential *pratimas* are: right vision, observing the twelve vows (*anuvratas, gunavratas* and *siksavratas*), practising equanimity, concentration on the self, maintaining a weekly fast, avoiding the use of animate objects, abstinence from eating at night, complete celibacy, renunciation of all worldly occupations, all worldly concerns and finally, the renunciation of the world as an ascetic. It is ultimately the ascetic, saint or muni, who can aspire to final emancipation.

The word *moksha* is derived from the Sanskrit verbal root *mus*, which literally means 'release' or 'to set free'. Monier Monier Williams in his Sanskrit-English dictionary has explained this state as an eradication of all passions (*kleshas*) and cravings (*trishna*). The literal translation arrived at is 'blown out' or 'put out', 'extinguished'. It is the final release from matter and reunion with the supreme spirit. In religious terms, *moksha* denotes the ultimate release or spiritual liberation from conditioned existence or *samsara*. Alternatively, it may be considered a metaphysical concept denoting the state of supreme peace and final beatitude. Indian sacred literature across traditions is replete with synonyms of *moksha* — *mukti, siddhi, nirvana, bodhi, kaivalya* are just a few of them. One who has attained the final goal, the end of all sufferings — one who does not come again to this world and is above all good and evil, is said to have achieved *moksha*.

In Jainism, *moksha* describes the liberation of the self from the snares of karma. It is the complete separation from all those impurities which curtail and hinder the self's natural qualities. In the metaphysical sense, it is the realization of the self by the self — the cessation of suffering, where there is neither birth nor death, decay nor disease, contact nor separation. All evil has waned, all weaknesses been torn out; the soul has done all that was to be done, known all that was to be known. This state is an extremely pure one, in which the soul attains unthinkable attributes of knowledge and bliss. The existence of the self in its pure form and forever is *moksha*. The liberated *Jiva* always remains in the *siddhashila* (the abode of the perfected souls) never returning to *samsara*. It exists unexcelled for all eternity, endowed with unending and unsurpassed bliss.

The Gommatasara has actually spelled out the eight qualities that the liberated self possesses: perfect knowledge (*kevalajnana*), perfect perception (*kevaladarsana*), infinite power (*anantavirya*), perfect belief (*samyaktva*), imperturbability (*avyavadha*), extreme fineness (*suksmatva*), interpenetrability (*avaghanatva*), and neither low nor high, neither heavy nor light (*agurrulaghu*). The last is somewhat unclear. Jaina tradition acknowledges three different categories of enlightened beings: *arahats, tirthankaras* and *siddhas*.

Just as it is difficult to precisely explain the state achieved during perfect meditation — it is something that only the meditator realizes by himself — so also is the explanation of *moksha* beyond verbal expression. This is probably why, wherever the term occurs in spiritual texts, a generally negative expression of the concept is dwelled upon. Even the Acharangasutra states that "he perceives, he knows but there is no analogy."

Finding Purpose in the Flow

Nergis Dalal

In his book, *Flow: The Psychology of Happiness,* Mihaly Csikszentmihalyi claims that decades of research on the positive aspects of human experience have proved that what makes any experience genuinely satisfying and enjoyable is a state of mind in which attention is totally concentrated. In this state, the self feels free and un-selfconscious and in effortless control. Emotional problems disappear and one's abilities are at their peak. A state of transcendence or flow has been achieved. This is the 'autotelic experience', in which the experience is not a means to a reward, but is its own end and reward. The word 'autotelic' is a combination of two Greek words, autos (meaning self) and telos (meaning goal). In an autotelic state, the activity, project or experience in which the self is involved is a self-contained, pleasurable and totally satisfying condition. A flow exists when the concentration is so complete that there is no attention left over to think about anything irrelevant, or to worry about problems.

Painters, writers, musicians or chess players can be so absorbed in their creative efforts that, for them, time is completely distorted — in fact, time ceases to exist for them. But the same exalted state of being can be experienced by engineers, doctors, scientists, soldiers, athletes, rock- and mountain-climbers and even by technicians working in a factory.

The difference is not between one kind of activity and another, but between the degree of experiential intensity obtained by one engaged in an activity, whether 'special' or 'ordinary'. All of us are free to use our limited attention, after all, in one of two ways: either by focusing it intentionally like a beam of energy or, alternatively, by diffusing it in random movements. The shape and content of our lives depend on how our attention has been used. We create ourselves by depending on how we invest this energy. Attention and personal goals are the most important tools in the task of improving the quality of experience. As Saint-Beuve wrote: "I am only fulfilled when, pen in hand, I sit in the silence of my room."

The human nervous system is so complex that a person can make himself happy or miserable, regardless of what is happening outside of himself, simply by changing his consciousness. What we think, feel, see and desire is information that we can manipulate and use. Consciousness can be thought of as intentionally ordered information.

Too many of us end up feeling that we have wasted our lives and that, instead of happiness and fulfillment, we are mired in boredom, anxiety and depression. "How we feel about ourselves, the joy we get from living, ultimately depends directly on how the mind filters and interprets everyday experiences. The universe is not hostile, nor yet is it friendly. It is simply indifferent" is an insight that many of us have yet to internalize.

So how then can we live joyfully and creatively in an indifferent universe? The only way to do this is to control consciousness and restructure it. We waste too much psychic energy trying to impress others or even influence them. Whatever we do should itself actively be the reward. Autotelic personalities are strongly directed towards purpose, where energy is free and not constricted by thoughts of the self. For such people, opportunities for action and advancement will always be present. The Taoist scholar Chuang Tzu observed that the right way to live was to flow spontaneously, without hoping for rewards, yet moving with total commitment. This flow is characterized by a feeling that one's skills are adequate to cope with challenges in a goal-oriented system, which, along the way, provides clues to how one is performing. "The autotelic self transforms potentially entropic experience into flow by setting clear goals, becoming immersed in the activity, concentrating on what is happening and learning to enjoy immediate experiences," writes Csikszentmihalyi.

To set goals, to develop skills, to focus attention and to be totally involved — these lead not only to fulfillment but often to outstanding achievement. The autotelic personality does not wish to dominate the environment. It finds a way to live harmoniously with and within it. People who are successful generally enjoy what they are doing: self-registered goals, when concentrated upon to the limit, produce a flow in which new skills can be developed, psychic energy increased and actions are integrated into a unified purpose — this is what we mean when we speak of `a meaning to life'.

Love 24X7 Takes you to the State of Everlasting Joy

Thich Nhat Hanh

Four important subjects are discussed in the Samiddhi Sutra: the idea of happiness, the existence of real joy, the practice of reliance, and the trap of complexes. Our notions about happiness entrap us. We forget that they are just ideas. Our idea of happiness can prevent us from actually being happy. The second idea is that of the existence of real joy. When a goddess asked the young monk Samiddhi why he chose to abandon happiness in the present moment for a vague promise of happiness in the future, Samiddhi answered, "The opposite is true. It is the idea of happiness in the future that I have abandoned, so I can dwell deeply in the present moment." The third topic the Sutra discusses is the practice of reliance, or support. Relying on Dharma is not just an idea. When you live in accordance with the Dharma, you realize joy, tranquillity, stability, and freedom. It is 'taking refuge in the island of self', the island of peace in each of us. We must know how to return to that island when we need to. In his last moments, the Buddha said, "Take refuge in the island of self... There you will find Buddha, Dharma, and Sangha." The fourth subject concerns the trap of complexes — thinking you are better, worse than, or equal to others. The complexes arise because we think we are a separate self. Happiness built on the notion of a separate self is weak and unreliable. Through the practice of meditation, we come to see that we 'inter-are' with all other beings, and our fears, anxieties, anger, and sorrow disappear. If you practise true happiness, relying on the Dharma and realizing the interconnected and interdependent nature of all things, you become freer and more stable every day. Gradually you will be in a paradise where the deep love described by the Buddha pervades.

Happiness is not an individual matter; it has the nature of interbeing. When you are able to make one friend smile, her happiness will nourish you also. When you find ways to peace, joy, and happiness, you do it for everyone. Begin by nourishing yourself with joyful feelings. Practise walking meditation outside, enjoying the fresh air, the trees, the stars in the night sky. What do you do to nourish yourself ? It is important to discuss this subject with dear friends to find concrete ways to nourish joy and happiness. When you succeed in doing this, your suffering, sorrow, and painful mental formations will begin to transform. When your body is invaded by harmful bacteria, your own antibodies surround the bacteria and render them harmless. When there aren't enough antibodies, your body will create more so it can neutralize the infection. Likewise, when you suffuse your body and mind with feelings of the joy of meditation, your body and spirit will be strengthened. Joyous feelings have a capacity to transform the feelings of sorrow and pain in us.

The Buddha's teachings on love are clear. It is possible to live 24 hours a day in a state of love. The Four Immeasurable Minds are strong concentrations of love, compassion, joy and equanimity. When you dwell in these concentrations, you are living in the most beautiful, peaceful, and joyous realm in the universe.

Knowledge, not Experience, is Path to Anubhava

Swami Dayananda

ow can happiness be experienced? Whenever you pick up a resolving moment of happiness you experience your essential self. Through some gain, sensation, a profound appreciation of beauty, whatever, a certain mental condition occurs in which for the moment you are just with yourself. In the quiet clarity of a mind that wants no change whatsoever, you pick up a moment of *ananda*. You do not recognize that *ananda* as yourself; you attribute it to an object or a situation experienced.

Desiring *ananda* all the time, you continually seek it through all your actions. Nobody desires something that is unknown. You know what *ananda* is and that is why you want it. What you do not know is that you are *ananda*; you cannot help but seek it because it is your very nature and you cannot settle for anything else, for anything less. But you do know there is such a thing as *ananda*; that there are moments of fullness which are moments of happiness.

Even if you gain new experience which reveals *ananda* to you, it makes no difference. Whether the experiences you have are usual or unusual, they still have to be assimilated in terms of knowledge. Experience by itself does not give knowledge for experience. It comes and goes. Vedanta provides the basis for knowledge that the moment of happiness I experience reflects my real nature, *ananda*, limitlessness, fullness. Knowledge of the whole that frees me. For that knowledge, I need to know what is *mithya,* apparently real, and what is *satyam,* non-negatable reality. I have to account for this world or else things will not fall into place. Just slipping into myself is not enough. If I do not discover the nature of the world and that of myself the world will overwhelm me and I will have to escape.

Vedanta has been erroneously presented as an experience. Vedanta is knowledge, not a happening; it is the immediacy of knowledge. When that immediacy of knowledge is presented as experience, confusion follows in part because the Sanskrit word, *anubhava* has been translated in English simply as 'experience'. This causes the expectation of a 'happening', not a 'seeing'. *Anubhava* is immediate knowledge. That which is in keeping with the teaching is called *anubhava*. That which comes after the teaching is knowledge in keeping with the teaching. 'Experience' is immediate knowledge.

Is happiness 'realization' rather than 'experience'?

It is recognition in terms of knowledge. You recognize the truth of yourself in terms of knowledge — a knowledge that embraces you, your world, and God. In knowledge you see the non-dual as a whole. Experience is only an escape from the perception of duality; knowledge accounts for duality. In knowledge I face duality and see there is no duality. I appreciate and enjoy the world I perceive; at the same time I know there is no duality. Knowledge requires a *pramana*, an instrument of knowledge and someone to wield that instrument. Shruti, scripture, is the *pramana* and the teacher wields the *pramana*, unfolding the words of Shruti until the student sees the fact of the whole and knows, 'That whole I am'.

Logical Deduction for Happiness in Life

Ramesh Balsekar

Daily living has three aspects:

1) Each individual has a particular situation; this means deciding what you want in a given situation and doing whatever you think you should do to get it. Once you have done it, your free will has ended.

2) What happens after is not in your control. Experience shows that sometimes you have got what you wanted and sometimes you have not. Or what you have got has been totally unexpected, for better or worse.

3) Thereafter, society accepts what has actually happened as your own action, good or bad, and you are rewarded or punished.

Reward has come to mean pleasure and punishment has come to be understood as pain, all in the moment. We have no choice but to accept if we want to continue living in that society. This constitutes your happiness or unhappiness from moment to moment over which you have no control, nor can you know what will bring pleasure or pain, or know the total amount of pleasure and pain assigned to you during your lifetime. Happiness cannot depend on what you experience moment to moment. Therefore, happiness must depend upon your attitude to life. It is important that you engage yourself in self-enquiry: What is your attitude to life that has prevented you from being happy? The main reason for our unhappiness is your relationship with the other. Daily living means your relationship with the other — whether the other is a close relative, a colleague at work or a total stranger. You cannot be happy unless your relationship with the other is harmonious. Being happy is to be at peace with yourself, that is, never to be uncomfortable with yourself. You are not totally comfortable with yourself in your relationship with the other because the other will not always do what you want him to do, and, you cannot expect him to do that either! Does it mean that we can never be happy? That's not true because we know at least one or two people who enjoy the same pleasures we do, suffer the same pain, and yet they are transparently happy, never uncomfortable with themselves.

Another problem is apparently a dead end. The third force is the concept offered by the Buddha. You cannot expect the other always to do what you want him to do. No one really does anything. Events happen, deeds are done, consequences happen, but no one does any deed. Everything happens according to a Cosmic Law; how each happening affects whom in what way — for better or worse — is also according to Cosmic Law; therefore, no one can be blamed for any happening. Everything is a happening for which neither you nor the other can be blamed. So even if a happening hurts, you cannot hate anyone, neither yourself nor the other. With the total acceptance of this concept, in an instant, your load of hatred for yourself (for your actions) and the load of hatred for the other disappears. The absence of this load of hatred — both for yourself and for others — is the presence of peace of mind for yourself and a harmonious relationship with the other: The happiness you have been seeking all your life.

For Happy Living Follow Two Rules

L Ron Hubbard

There are two rules which, when followed, can greatly help one to get along with others. These are the two rules for happy living: First, to be able to experience anything, and second, cause only those things which others are able to experience easily.

The maxim 'Do unto others as you would have others do unto you' has been repeated often in various religions. But such golden rules, while they served to help human beings rise above base instincts, resulted in no sure sanity, success or happiness. Such a golden rule gives only the cause-point, or at best the reflexive effect-point. This is a self-done-to-self concept and tends to put one on an obsessive cause. It gives no thought to what one does about the things others not so indoctrinated do to us.

How should we handle the unsavoury things others do to us? There are many random answers to this question: that the effects on self don't exist; become a martyr; condemn all sin; and so on. But they are incomplete. How to be happy is a subject few have ventured to address directly. They only assure us that as human beings, we are doomed to suffer, so they tell us not how to be happy, but how to endure being unhappy. We have a negative goal: to get rid of all the unhappiness on Earth so that it is made livable. If you seek to get rid of something continually, you admit that you are unable to confront it.

The effect side of life deserves great consideration. The self-caused side also deserves examination. To create only those effects which others could easily experience gives us a new rule of living. If you examine your life, you will find you are bothered only by those actions a person did which others were not able to receive. The more actions a person generates which could not be experienced by others, the worse a person's life became.

Communication is one means of reaching others. If a person is unable to communicate, he won't really get to know about others; and with knowing little or nothing about others, he doesn't have any feeling about them either, thus his affinity will be low. Affinity, reality and communication work together; and if one of these three is high, the other two will also be high; but if one is low, so will others be. All bad acts, then, are those acts, which cannot be easily experienced at the target end.

By this definition, let us review our own 'bad acts'. Which ones were bad? Only those that could not be easily experienced by another were bad. Thus, which of society's favourite bad acts are bad? Acts of real violence resulting in pain, unconsciousness, insanity and heavy loss could at this time be considered bad. The things which you have done which you could not easily, yourself, experience were bad. But the things which you have done which you, yourself, could have experienced, had they been done to you, were not bad. That certainly changes one's view of things!

There is no need to lead a violent life just to prove one can experience. The idea is not to prove one can experience, but to regain the ability to experience. We now have two golden rules for happiness: Be able to experience any thing; and cause only those things which others are able to experience easily. Your reaction to these tells how far you have yet to go. And if you achieve these two golden rules, you would be one of the happiest and most successful people in this universe.

Less Possessions, More Happiness

Anil K Rajvanshi

A well-to-do disciple was very fond of his frugal guru who used to live in a remote village, meditating under a tree most of the time. The guru was a free bird; he had neither family nor home. He sustained himself by begging for alms. There were days when he even went without food, but that did not seem to bother him. He was focused on his meditation and ascetic lifestyle. The fact that such a learned and good man had no regular livelihood — and so did not know where his next meal was coming from — bothered the disciple. After some thought he decided that he would give his guru a cow so that he would not have to depend on the charity of others for food. He would have to beg no more. The guru, however, refused the gift saying that he was very happy with his existence. Also, since he had taken to a frugal way of life in order to direct his energies to spiritual pursuits, he would rather not get into the trap of acquiring worldly possessions. Nevertheless, after great persuasion and cajoling, he reluctantly accepted the cow. The disciple was delighted and felt that he had done a great service to his guru.

Many years passed before the disciple returned to the village to seek advice from his guru. Not finding him under the tree he inquired about his whereabouts from the villagers. They pointed at a hamlet in the distance. He went there. Seeing the disciple, the guru rushed out from one of the huts and wailed: "Look how you have ruined my life... First the cow, then the cowgirl and the rest followed! I cannot meditate and most of my time goes in running this outfit."

Possessions burden your mind and are a distraction to deep thought. Thinking of ways on how to acquire more, the pursuit of possessions becomes an end in itself. Similarly, there is a tendency in people to amass wealth for the sake of hoarding it. It is of no use to anyone. This becomes a way of life. Possessions and wealth are necessary for a comfortable life. However, they should serve our need, not greed. Whether it is clothing, shoes or homes, possessing more than what is required is nothing but wasteful hoarding. Amassing of wealth and possessions comes from internal insecurity of an individual. This leads to a spiral: to get more money for acquiring more goods and services, often leading to a corrupt and unsustainable lifestyle.

This insecurity can be reduced by first trying to understand ourselves. Most people are afraid of looking deep within. But a deeper understanding will give us a perspective in life and is the genesis of spirituality, it will help in the understanding of the spirit inside us.

Spirituality can also help in keeping our greed for materials and resources in check. As a person progresses on the path of spirituality his or her priorities in life change. The focus of life shifts more towards getting personal happiness through mental peace and is less on material needs and desires and hence towards sustainability. Spirituality also helps make a person internally secure and humble.

Since the desire to increase possessions and amass wealth comes from the greed impulse it should be reduced or kept in check. Removal of greed can be achieved by cultivating a spiritual outlook with the help of yoga and *sanyam*. The brain has tremendous processing power and hence even a small amount of data is processed efficiently to gain useful information. This helps the mind to 'get satisfied' easily so that the person can move on. Reduction and ultimately the complete removal of greed is the key to happiness and sustainability.

I am not Suffering, I am Happiness

Vinay Kamat

They call me Suffering. I know everyone. But they don't know me enough. I feel it's time to tell my story. Don't worry, it's not an autobiography. It's a desire to express myself, truly and entirely. Before I do that, I must say that I have been impressed by Turkish writer Orhan Pamuk's style of making emotion speak for itself. So, I would like to reveal myself by engaging You deeply.

Let me begin with my birth. I was born as Happiness. I was renamed Suffering by a world that could not see beyond Existence — its immediate concerns. I bear no grudges. After all, philosophers have sensed my duality, recognizing Happiness as my other manifestation. Others have tried to deconstruct duality to understand me better, and failed. How can you simplify duality? How can I exist as Good and Bad at the same time? How can I even be Positive or Negative? Call me what you want. I have no opposites. I have no similarities. I have no likes. I have no dislikes.

A poet has said Suffering is the only genuine feeling. Anything that is genuine and pure is unattached, unengaged, free, blithe. Then, why do I suffer the misinterpretation of my identity? I am neither Happiness nor Suffering. I am life's sustenance, its continuity. I am not a whim, a mood, or a tsunami. It's only human to see me as such. Sometimes it's refreshing to pick up a slice of conversation that tells you more about yourself. I was the subject of a recent discussion at a New Year get-together. It was quite a revelation to listen to a couple talk about me.

The girl said, "Suffering is not plight. It's an evolution that strengthens resolve. It's not just enlightenment. It's purification of emotion. Christ ennobled us when he said, 'Father forgive them, for they know not what they do'. Arthur Ashe forgot he had AIDS when he remembered the good things that he had had as the world's top tennis player. He saw no reason to blame God. Malaysian political leader Anwar Ibrahim transcended suffering by refusing to be angry about it. Even in his agony, he believed in trust."

I was beginning to enjoy the conversation. Her partner responded: "Suffering is an awakening. The 'I' (the individual) suffers because it refuses to reconcile itself with the cosmic 'All' (the larger good). Indeed, the 'I' must not reconcile; it must become one with the all-embracing 'All'. In so doing, it liberates itself from Suffering; its isolation ceases. In the vastness of its being and the nothingness of its purpose, the 'All' senses no emotion."

I was about to interrupt when the girl spoke: "Continuity has no consequence. Where there's no consequence, how can there be Suffering? Suffering is a continuum, like Life. It's a stream where Happiness, Sorrow, Guilt, Compassion and Empathy are the reflexes of the swimmer (the individual)."

It was a profound conversation. But I have yet to make my point. I have tried to fathom my duality; I have questioned people who still call me Suffering; I have suffered in silence. I have wondered whether Karna was cruel, compassionate, or carefree. I have read *The Da Vinci Code* and wondered why it had no grim or happy ending. As I looked around for answers, I found some in myself. To say that Suffering is an inexplicable, multifaceted, never-ending, story is to be simplistic. I am much more than that. I make people happy despite me. I break their bonds with the 'I'. I am Happiness.

Happiness Lies in Mind Control

Shri Aasaramji Bapu

Never has the young generation experienced so much chaos as in current times. Media, politicians, terrorists, educationists, missionaries and saints — all have made them their common target. Good and evil, fanatics and moderates, all wish the youth to agree with their point of view. For a country, it is of utmost importance that the youth are looked after in terms of mental, psychological and spiritual development. Any wrong education imparted to them can be dangerous for all humanity.

Very few can resist the ceaseless thoughts and desires that pass their mind. Words have immense power to invoke violence in the young, the sight of so many luxuries excites them, negative thoughts are detrimental to their psychology. Curbing desire seems pointless to them. With little control over their senses, the young wish to fulfil all that their mind desires. Thwarted in this, they often resort to crime. Adding fuel to fire are those who advise them to listen to their heart's dictates. Ideals are mocked at. The contemporary mantra is to let the senses rule the intellect. The result is increase in crime, loss of tolerance and an erosion of moral values.

The age from 12 years to 25 years is the most dangerous. Energy levels are at their highest, hormonal changes take place, sensual pleasures take precedence over all else. Aware of the fire of the senses, *rishis* and *munis* dealt with such problems scientifically. They analysed that when energy is concentrated in the sexual organs or *mulaadhar*, it creates havoc in the body. This energy needs to be brought upwards towards the Shiva *netra*, which is in the middle of the brow. In yogic parlance, it is called Aagya Chakra. Also called the third eye, this point disciplines the mind and curtails negative emotions. Just as an airport needs a control tower, similarly the body needs an activated Aagya Chakra to control the mind. If it remains undeveloped it gives rise to an imbalance of emotions and a criminal bent of mind.

An activated Aagya Chakra improves concentration, develops inner discipline and negates negativity. Yogis devised several techniques to control the mind, but even among them few are able to conquer it. The mind is in constant danger from anger, ego, lust, attachment and pride. The more a person indulges in luxuries, the more he becomes intolerant and a slave of the mind. A yogi has learnt that the mind will be still only when it is one with inner light. It pains him to see the magnificent power of the mind going to senseless waste.

Vedanta had emphasized that outside elements play havoc with the mind. The only solution was disciplining of senses. Imitating their elders, the young feel no moral compunction in indulging the senses. Being full of energy, the young wish to conquer the world. A laudable goal, perhaps, but Vedanta says that this can be done only if you are in total control of your mind. Once you are free from slavery of the mind, no outside element can act upon you.

When a sage asks you to remain in touch with your culture he doesn't want to turn the clock backwards. When you go out from your home every morning don't you come back? When you rise don't you go to sleep at night? No one is stopping you from going out in the world, working hard and becoming wealthy. But, it is necessary to return to your consciousness after a hard day's work to find out whether you have strayed or led a life as stated by those ancient masters — the *rishis* and *munis*.

Irrespective of outer circumstances, one can be calm and quiet. There are plenty of yogic exercises that can tame the mind. The youth of today have great opportunities, and are able to procure wealth far sooner than their parents did. If spent nobly, wealth can be a blessing for humanity. The rule to happiness is in understanding your relationship with the world. *Sarve Bhavantu Sukhinah*: the entire universe should be happy.

Follow Dharma to Attain Bliss

Shri Maheswar Pathak

Dharma is essentially the path a man should follow for reaching the abode of God, the final destination of all life. Hinduism says that our abode is located in the 'land of God' but that we have been sentenced to a life of exile in this *samsara* or material world, because of our *karma* — the accumulated price of selfish actions carried out in millions of our past lives. *Samsara* is an ocean of 'death' where myriad beings are dying every moment and from which no being, however, high and mighty can escape. In other words, the material world has been called an ocean of misery. Due to all-pervasive death, happiness in *samsara* is as contradictory as 'hot ice'.

Everyone is, however, constantly striving to avoid misery and attain a state of bliss or everlasting peace and happiness. Avoiding misery is impossible without overcoming death or attaining immortality. Death cannot be averted without stopping the cycle of rebirths and rebirth ceases only upon attainment enlightenment or becoming one with God. In the *Bhagvad Gita* Sri Krishna says, "Having come to Me, these great souls do not get back to rebirth, the place of sorrow impermanent, for they have reached the highest perfection."

The essence of God is the seat of immortality, the abode of peace and happiness in the quest of which man has been eternally wandering in this universe. Reaching the abode of God therefore becomes the supreme goal of a person's life and the path of travel to God lies only in the field of dharma. The word Bhagavata has a twofold meaning — firstly, it represents the Bhagavata Purana — the crest jewel of puranic literature and secondly, it refers to the devotees of Sri Krishna. Bhagavata Dharma thus represents the road map to the abode of God as depicted in the Srimad Bhagavata or as shown by the devotees of the Lord Krishna through examples of their lives. The most striking feature of the Bhagavata Dharma is to regard the universe as God. Accordingly, the Bhagavata exhorts that the sun, the moon, the stars, the sky, the rivers, mountains, trees, animals, men, gods, the saint, the sinner, the ugly, the beautiful, the rich, the poor — should be worshipped as God.

Surrendering all of one's works — *laukika* or *vaidika* to God is another hallmark of the Bhagavata Dharma. Actions like seeing, hearing, walking, eating, speaking and thinking done according to the dictates or for enjoyment of the senses pertain to *laukika* while those acts and rituals performed according to the *sastras* or scriptures, normally to attain prosperity constitute the *vaidika*. Surrendering of work to God means performing a work or act with the idea that one is doing the same for satisfying God and not due to his own self-interest.

The supreme ideal of the Bhagavata Dharma is, however, *bhakti* or devotion to Lord Krishna. In fact, *bhakti* is the central theme in this dharma; it is actually the doorway to the abode of God. The *Gita* says that, "through devotion he comes to know me, what my measure is and who am I in truth; then having known me in truth he forthwith enters into me."

A question now arises as to where the abode of Lord Krishna is located. The Vedanta says that God abides only in the heart of the being and nowhere else — *jyotiratmani nanyatra*. For meeting God, one had therefore to enter into his own heart. Journey to the heart is however obstructed by a screen of impurities created by egotism which gives rise to desire for the enjoyment of senses. *Bhakti* is the only means of removing this screen. The Bhagavata posits nine kinds of bhakti out of which *sravana* and *kirtana* are considered the best. *Sravana* means hearing about the qualities and works of Lord Krishna from a true *vaisnava* who is to be regarded and served as a guru, and *kirtana* refers to singing the glories of the Lord as heard from the guru. These would gradually remove the impurities of one's heart and when these impurities are totally removed, Lord Krishna becomes manifest in one's heart in the same way as the sun behind the clouds appears in the sky when the clouds disappear. Such manifestation of Sri Krishna in one's heart is the fulfilment of the Bhagavata Dharma.

Lasting Happiness Comes from within

Harsh Kabra

The driving force behind every individual's worldly pursuit is a craving for mental peace and material pleasure. The yearning is for happiness that can weather the vicissitudes of the material world; happiness that is self-sustaining and that which cannot be impeded even by the strongest resistance. This longing for happiness is founded on definite expectations that revolve around intuitive happiness that is integral to the being. The experience is akin to the intuition of the chilly feeling that grows upon us as soon as we enter a snowy region. Or like a desert, nearing which we experience the intensity of heat and light. Likewise, the insurmountable pleasure embodied by the pursuit and realization of the Almighty inspires an emotion of happiness that is overwhelming and results in the culmination of self-discovery. One might then ask — notwithstanding the pursuit of the Almighty that all of us embark upon out of the fear of an uncertain future and the need for an instrument to extricate us from the troughs of despair — why does happiness continue to elude us?

As revealed in the *Bhagavad Gita*: Whenever the wavering heart wanders away, then so often let him subdue it and bring it back to the control of the soul; for supreme happiness comes to the *yogin* whose heart is at rest, in whom passion is tranquillized, who is one with Brahma, and free from sin.

At the root of our inability to merit happiness figure our extrovert minds and senses. These prevent us from experiencing the happiness borne out of the realization of the divine. They distract us from the most superior of aspirations of being one with the self to win over all battles within and without. This brings us to the next important question: is it possible in the present times with all its dilemmas to fulfil this aspiration? What physical and spiritual conquests hold out the promise of headway?

We need an escort while trekking, climbing peaks and traversing forests so that he anticipates and solves on our behalf all likely obstacles and setbacks we are likely to face during our journey. An escort becomes indispensable only by virtue of his familiarity with the path leading up to our destination. Similarly, the feeling of God's presence as an escort ameliorates the difficult path of the spiritual seeker, making his advance appear effortless. The mere assurance of an escort personifying strength, vigour, enterprise and success makes difficult situations endurable. Shallow waters cannot be used for an invigorating dip or for cultivation of crops. It is a prerequisite to conserve that water for instance by building a dam, with virtues of human effort to augment its depth and thereby its potential. The ability to shore up the unyielding flow of thoughts helps increase the mind's power of perception and hence the potential to benefit one and all.

It is important to rid the mind of material pleasures to make place for happiness. Just like one does not have a robust appetite during an ailment, the appetite to explore truth and discover the true self cannot be sustained with an ailing mind cluttered with transient and fruitless concerns. Lord Krishna tells Arjuna that a selfish medium lacks a lasting purpose in the scheme of this world. Hence happiness that emanates from dilution of the self is lasting in nature. This dilution is irreversible like a crystal of salt or sugar that, after dissolving in water, becomes irretrievable. This selfless state of the mind cannot be generically defined, but is characterized by the absence of anger and frustration. Lord Krishna himself admitted the inability to objectively define this state of mind. But the expression of spiritual gratification does not depend on the vocabulary of words, it can well articulate itself through the powerful sound of silence and intrinsic quietude woven by the strength of piety.

Kabir believed that the undoing of knots of ignorance and internal contradictions is God's greatest blessing to us. This explains in significant measure the power of restraint of mental and sensual traits in helping us fathom the depths of happiness by drowning in it the self-created dilemmas of life.

Discover the Secret of Happiness within

Deepak Nigam

In life everyone ceaselessly acts pursuing various goals. In and through all such pursuits one is ultimately seeking nothing but happiness. But are we clear about what happiness is, where to seek it and how to achieve it? Real happiness is an equanimous state of mind, when thoughts are at rest. It is a state of cessation of agitations, which are caused by unfulfilled desires of the mind. Desire is the thick stream of indiscriminate thought flow in you, drawn towards the world of objects and beings. You entertain desires within to fill the VOID or overcome the sense of unfulfilment you feel within you. To quieten these agitations caused by unfulfilled desires, we go through a variety of experiences at the physical, mental and intellectual levels of our personality. We contact objects, beings, emotions and thoughts of the world and try to find fulfilment in them, e.g. a child with toys, youth with wealth and women, the elderly in a newspaper and old friends. If our desires are fulfilled we are happy and if not we are in sorrow. But as George Bernard Shaw rightly said, "Man has to face two tragedies in life, one when his desire is fulfilled and the other when it is not." In both cases he ultimately faces mental agitations, in one case it's early and in the other it's later on.

The world is in a constant flux of change. The experiences of this world are passing and fleeting. And the happiness derived from the world of objects, emotions and thoughts is thus also passing in nature. For example, joy derived from an ice cream lasts only for a while. An old man reads a book or newspaper, which absorbs him for a few hours only. So, worldly happiness is not permanent. Therefore, lacking the knowledge of true happiness and its source, one focuses on the world to provide us with true happiness. But that results in experiencing instant joys followed by emptiness, sorrow and suffering. A young man plucked a beautiful rose to enjoy its fragrance. When he brought the rose in contact with his nose to enjoy its fragrance, a bee inside the rose suddenly stung him on the tip of his nose. The man cried in pain and the rose fell from his hand. In reality there is not a rose of 'sensual pleasure' that does not have the bee of 'injury' concealed in it.

Indiscriminate pursuit of pleasure objects invariably comes up against the law of neutralization. It is the state where any further contact with the objects gives no more happiness, whereas its absence creates sorrow. A person in the midst of riches and plenty may remain dull and bored, yet the absence of these would generate sorrow. A regular alcoholic in contact with alcohol gets no pleasure but abstinence from it brings him suffering.

True happiness, we should realize, does not belong to the realm of the physical, emotional or intellectual levels of our personality. It belongs to our true nature. Beyond the levels of our body, mind and intellect lies our Real Self, our supreme nature, the source of infinite happiness, the Godhead in us. Christ said, "The kingdom of heaven lies within you. He who knoweth shall find it." And Guru Nanak said the same thing: "If you want permanent happiness, seek the Ram within you."

We don't have access to the Godhead within because it is veiled by our desires. In order to unveil our Real Self, Vedanta says that one must raise oneself above the desires. As long as one functions on desires, they multiply, which causes further mental agitations and stress. Instead, with the help of the intellect, one must channelize these desires to a higher ideal, towards an unselfish cause in life. Desires must neither be suppressed nor indulged in. Through discriminative control and channelizing, they get sublimated. As desires drop within us, there is increasing peace and happiness within our being. Vedanta provides us with the knowledge of life and living, the mental equipment to tackle life's problems, to always be happy and remain unaffected by sorrow. As one gets more and more subjective happiness, the less one is dependent on the external world for happiness. This everlasting happiness which lies right within the core of our heart, we search in vain in our outward experiences.

An old lady lost her needle in her cottage. It being dark inside she went out under the street lamp to search for it. So it is the case with most of us. We search externally while the kingdom of heaven lies right within us. Discover it. That is the secret of happiness.

No more Questions, only Bliss

RK Gupta

If there is one thing equally sought by all, it is happiness. All beings constantly endeavour to seek more happiness through new means of comfort. Science, religion and spirituality all aim at making human beings happier and, therefore, these are not contradictory paths that are at loggerheads with one another. The three paths are complimentary, being the essential attributes of the three dimensions of human existence, relating to body, mind and soul.

We have three kinds of bodies — the gross or physical body, the subtle or mental body also known as the psyche and the causal body or soul. When these three bodies combine, a new life is born. The causal body acts as storehouse of all action, thought and desire and causes the subtle body to combine with gross body, suitable to bear the fruit of what has been stored. It is like a software programme that is inscribed on the psyche for directing and guiding the physical body accordingly. The combining of the physical body and mental body is called birth and their separation is called death.

The characteristic qualities of physical body are movement and growth. Through its faculties of sight, hearing, smell, touch and taste, the physical body gathers impressions of things all around it. All things in the world are transitory in nature, continuously acquiring different forms and states of existence. The human body gathers impressions about them through the five senses. The knowledge that is gathered by the senses falls in the arena of science. Scientific knowledge is thus based on the analysis of information gathered by the senses, which can be subject to scrutiny and verification using physical means. This is why scientists find it difficult to believe in those things, which cannot be proved through experimentation or cannot be perceived through the senses.

Science presents us with various means of comfort for deriving happiness but true happiness really lies in the mind. A child derives immense pleasure from his toys. As he grows older, he loses interest in them and seeks new means of pleasure. It is not the objects but the state of mind that relates to true happiness. The mind is constantly fed by the senses. It receives impressions, stores them and reacts to them. If the mind is not focussed it does not register impressions.

The characteristic qualities of mind are thinking and knowing. All religions advise us to avoid vices and acquire virtues. The purpose of all religions is to train the mind so as to remain unaffected by the transitory nature of things. Religion teaches us to rise above pride and prejudices and to acquire equanimity so that we can understand and perceive things as they are. A stable mind, which has acquired equanimity, makes one really happy in all circumstances.

Spirituality means to know the real nature of things beyond their transitory nature. It leads to acquiring knowledge of the all-pervading Self and knowing the Self as the source of all happiness and bliss. Then, we come to the end of our quests. Knowledge is in discrimination, in distinguishing between different things or events. With Self-realization one attains the highest level of knowledge, of non-duality — that he himself is the source of all bliss. Thus concludes our search for happiness outside.

Self-awareness can Bring Happiness

Swami Bodhananda

The very concept of God has given rise to many theological disputes and religious warfare. In fact, God is an enduring in-depth experience in the midst of ever-changing mental and sensate experiences — God is the inexhaustible source of love, harmony and peace.

Happiness is sought by everyone. But the search is not focused in the right direction. We waste precious time seeking happiness in the mirage of objects, places and people; in relationships and ideologies; in possessions and wanton indulgences. Some seek happiness in caves, in mountains or on the shifting sands of deserts, practising severe penance. Our *rishis* called them extroverts — those who seek happiness in the objective domain with wasteful efforts, disregarding the subjective. In fact, happiness is a function of the subjective. But to seek happiness in the subjective domain is impossible, because the subjective can never become an object of seeking. That means to seek happiness in either direction is to miss happiness. That realization makes the seeker spontaneously detached, silent and contemplative. Meditation means all that. So meditation is the only door to happiness. Meditation means just 'to be happy'.

A group of American tourists were visiting Japan. They made it a point to visit as many Buddhist temples as possible and participate in all their religious practices. In one of those temples they were introduced to a Zen master. The Americans, puzzled by the rituals, said, "We visited many of your temples and participated in many of your practices, but we don't understand what your theology is." The Zen master roared with laughter: "We have no theology or philosophy, we simply laugh and dance."

Kavya Kanta Ganapathi Muni, a Vedic scholar and devotee of Shakti, once approached Ramana Maharshi and asked, "Bhagavan, what is true meditation?"

Maharshi said, "Watching the source of thought is meditation."

The source of thought is Self. Ignoring the Self is unhappiness. Being conscious of one's ignorance is meditation. Thought projects time veiling consciousness. Identifying with time is unconsciousness and the cause of suffering. Consciousness is bliss, which is transcendence of time. Consciousness is awareness of the self as the light in which thoughts, feelings and sensations shine and responses happen. How far is consciousness from the phenomenal world? How far is the Creator God from creation? Is bliss opposed to body experiences? Can happiness be an enduring experience in the ups and downs of actual living? Living in constant awareness of one's spiritual nature while interacting with the world is experiencing happiness moment to moment.

Sri Narayana Guru said, "To act with awareness is freedom and to act without awareness is bondage." The difference between freedom and bondage is awareness. Self-awareness is true awareness with reference to which the thought projected world is seen as a myth — as just a narration of an imaginative mind.

"Tell me," demanded the king, turning to his bewildered minister, waking up from an afternoon siesta. "Just a while ago I was a butterfly. Now, on waking up, I find myself to be a king. Which of these two experiences is the truth?"

The minister replied: "Your Highness, doubtless, you are king — not a butterfly." The king was not convinced.

He said, "O minister, how do you know? It might be that I am the king in the butterfly's dream!"

Happiness in every day life means walking wakefully in this dream world. Self-awareness helps find true happiness.

Siddha Maha Yoga can Bring about Positive Changes

AM Kulkarni

appiness is our timeless goal. Since we have a notion that anything pleasant or pleasurable to the senses would lead to happiness, our mind craves for such experiences. However, there are several shortcomings in seeking happiness this way.

Firstly, senses always require some external object in order to convey an experience. This spells 'dependence'. Secondly, experience of sense gratification is only temporary, while what we really are looking for is a lasting state. Thirdly, if an experience is pleasurable, the senses demand more of the same experience, leading to a constant state of wanting.

Yoga deals with searching for lasting, sense-free happiness and knowledge. Entire manifest Creation is a cause and effect hierarchy matrix in which our senses and mind are at the effect end. Since for lasting happiness, its source has to be free from the five senses, ascend this hierarchy and move towards the cause end. First find a force in this hierarchy which is superior to the mind so that we could hand over the mind along with all its disturbing contents to it. This superior force is our own *prana shakti*. It is *prana shakti* that decided and caused your body and also mind to take form and shape in the womb. It caused the first heartbeat and also your first breath and will continue so till death.

The self-intelligent *shakti* in Nature, which gives shape, form and mind, to the foetus, becomes dormant at birth as *shakti* has finished work till that point. Yogis named this dormant shakti as Kundalini *shakti*. After birth, as per the Law of Cause and Effect or Karma, the average person has to live out some or all of past karma in this lifespan. A person is hence born with a certain constitution, driven by subtle energy centres or *chakras* which are preset.

If, after having completed the task of creation or birth, had *shakti* not become dormant, she would have commenced her return journey towards Pure Consciousness and in effect, having to work through that person, would have rebalanced the *chakra* presets by means of causing various corrective *kriyas*, thus bypassing the need to actually live out the karma.

Most yoga practices directly or indirectly aim at balancing these energy *chakras* wilfully. You need to find out which one is suitable for you as every individual is constitutionally different, is at a different stage of evolution in terms of the journey towards the Absolute.

During daily Siddha Yoga Sadhana, all one has to do is to sit relaxed and simply surrender one's will to the awakened Kundalini *shakti* and be a calm witness as *prana shakti* works out various corrective *kriyas*. As a preparatory practice for Siddha Maha Yoga, one should begin by learning to hand over the mind, at least for a few minutes everyday, to this Mother Prana Shakti manifesting in all of us as breath.

The aspirant could make a start as outlined below:

1. Sit in a comfortable position, keeping the body loose and relaxed.
2. Close the eyes and become a calm witness to your natural breathing. 3. As soon as the eyes are closed, feel a current or a wave rising from the base of the spine to the top of the brain.
4. Practise this for five minutes or more.

Done regularly, the preparatory practice will result in many positive changes. It will also kindle one's wish to obtain grace from the right guide on this path. From then on, during daily *sadhana*, the awakened *prana shakti* will cause to remove all the physical, mental, emotional and spiritual imbalances within the *sadhaka*.

Happiness is not Everything

Swami Brahmdev

The idea of happiness is a kind of ignorance. If your understanding is healthy, then you will never give too much importance to happiness; we do so because of our ignorance. Happiness is not the idea, purpose or aim of life; happiness is a consequence, a fruit. Happiness is a subject of the senses. The scope of the senses is limited and the senses are completely unaware of the greatness of life. So if you are just following your senses, you are indulging them. You are just living with your senses.

Understand the game of the senses, and then go beyond them. Discover that portion of life, that part of life that can give us something permanent, the highest knowledge of life, the highest clarity in life. Nobody enters the path with full clarity, so even if you are ignorant or you lack the aspiration, somehow you will get connected. For instance, you have a certain understanding of life and what you want. On the basis of what you know, your highest goal is to find happiness. As you undergo experiences in the course of life, your understanding grows wider and deeper. You begin to see that happiness is not everything, that there is something beyond, that happiness comes and goes. You begin to think that perhaps satisfaction and being content is more important, no matter the kind of circumstances you are faced with. You could be content if you wished to be so.

Earlier your level of understanding prompted you to say, "How can I be content when I don't have this, or I don't have that?" Now your level of understanding has changed, and with that understanding you don't miss anything, you are fully content. If the understanding is high then you will not give too much importance to happiness, or sadness. When you aspire for something higher you will give more importance to your clarity, to your higher understanding, you will live for that; you will not give importance to whether the path is long or not, you will not give importance to the path at all, you will give importance to the target, the target is higher, aspiration is higher.

When you climb a mountain with the aim of reaching the top you have clarity. You know that you have to reach the top. That clarity helps you. The path will be very difficult, and maybe you will not be happy on the way, but when you reach the top that will give you much more than happiness, it will give you contentment. If we are only looking for happiness then we will never be able to climb high, aim high, or aspire for anything that can help us to evolve further. What we understand by happiness lies on the surface. When you live at a deeper level, you give importance to clarity of consciousness which gives you information on the purpose of your existence; it gives you purpose. Once this is clear everything will come to you, including contentment and balance.

Contentment is the Kernel of Happiness

Sukhvinder Singh

abir highlighted the importance of *santosha* or contentment in our lives. Indian culture teaches us to be content in all situations. But today, we are not happy with the grades our child gets, our pay packet, our spouse, or our ageing parents. Much of the stress in our lives is the result of our inability to be content with what we have.

The natural and healthy growth of children is hampered by unreasonable expectations of parents. A child is a gift of God and should be allowed to grow like a sapling. All saplings do not grow to the same height nor do they produce flowers of equal size and shape. Like a mountain stream, a child must be allowed to chart her own course in life. Any attempt to alter or modify her natural course would curtail spontaneity. It is better to allow one's child to be and let her enjoy life rather than coerce her to do what she does not like.

Materialism begets needless unhappiness. The failure to live within one's means leads to unprecedented corruption in all walks of life. Unlimited income, more often than not, leads to indulgence and ill-health and there can be no happiness in the absence of good health. It is essential that an individual plans his expenditure and is satisfied with his income. A portion of one's income must be set aside for charity to help the less privileged. It is not without reason that charity is given a place of prominence in all religions. Contentment and charity go hand in hand.

Nowadays, marriages increasingly end in acrimony and divorce. Earlier, couples were content; they made space for each other, perhaps also because of the joint family tradition. To forge a successful relationship, it is essential to accept perceived shortcomings of a spouse and work together towards self-improvement by helping each other in times of distress. By concentrating on the good qualities of one's partner, one can rescue floundering relationship.

Following the disintegration of the joint family loneliness in old age has become a cause for concern. Loneliness becomes doubly painful after loss of a life partner in old age. But upon some reflection, it would appear that loneliness can be translated into solitude. A number of people, the young included, take to the hills in search of solitude.

Therefore, it is important to accept loneliness and turn it into solitude instead of entertaining expectations from children. The renowned Sufi poet Bulle Shah asked his spiritual guide why he was unable to concentrate on anything. The latter who was planting onion saplings uprooting them from one place only to plant them again in another place, said, *"Bulleya man da ki samjhauna edhron putna odhar launa* (Bulleya, it is only a question of making your mind understand shifting it from one issue to another)."

In our old age we must shift our focus from our children to cultivate other interests such as the study of scriptures, yoga, travelling, *pranayama* and community service. One should prepare for this situation in life by taking occasional breaks from family ties even before old age comes upon us. Accepting the will of God *(Bhagwan ki marzi)* is another important aspect of Indian tradition. It is this spirit which helps the poorest of the poor to live cheerfully. To be content with one's lot and accept the will of God in difficult times helps in the attainment of peace and happiness. A lot of our discontent can be traced to the habit of making comparisons. Comparing one's income, child or spouse with others leads to unhappiness. Once we learn to be content we can be happy and stress free. Greed, and not need causes discontent. A need can be fulfilled, greed never.

It's Absolute Bliss, within & without

Purushottam Mahajan

Nothing exists apart from the Absolute. Yet, the Absolute, being transcendent, does not suffer from the limitations of the sense-organs, of attributes, of time. It is imperceivable, eternally pure, unqualified and is bliss. By knowing the Absolute everything is known, and fear and delusion remain no more. The ultimate resting place exists in the Absolute. It is the knowledge of the Absolute that brings about the fulfilment of the nature of man, and the desire for the experience of Being is characterized by peace.

The world we live in and the world we experience is deeply rooted in what we may call the dialectic or duality. It manifests its nature in terms of rise and fall, birth and death, cause and effect, one and many, here and there, knower and the known, I and you. It is the collectivity of countless dualities that make up the Being in constant flux.

There is nothing in this world that can be said to be permanent. Being subject to its inherent nature, the world is transient and infirm. Blessed are they with the gift of knowledge who realize the unity of Being in the midst of the world of dualities. The knower of the Absolute is one who realizes and experiences the same Reality in everything, who finds the presence of Being in life and death, in I and you, in here and there, in a drop of water and in the waters of an ocean, in a small pebble and a mountain, in one and many. He alone has merged himself in the samata-gnosis of the Absolute who experiences the absence of difference.

Gurudeva Mangatramji, a great saint of our times, has explained the basic characteristics of the one who is firmly established in the *samata* —knowledge of the Absolute. According to him, "The characteristics of the one who realized the evenness or equilibrium of Being are that he is no more tormented either by pleasures or by sorrows, the one in whom the desire for the fruit of action is totally absent, and remain always and constantly established in the presence of own-being. He is a person who has achieved the state of total dispassion, for his intellect always remains free from the influence of sense-organs, and experiences both inwardly and outwardly the presence of the self alone. Dualities no more affect him and he remains firmly established in the sameness of the self."

For the ignorant, the multitude of things is real, whereas the knower of the Absolute sees and experiences the presence of unity in the apparent difference. The ordinary person of common sense, being subject to space and time, remains bound to innumerable sense-experiences. He is unable to find the presence of unity in diversity; he is unable to discover the presence of Being in that which is outside of him. For ordinary men and women, the apparent world of objects is real, and their intellects remain confined to the surface of objective reality. Even the man of natural state can gain some intimations of the Absolute if he succeeds in stabilizing his unstable intellect.

Only a mind that has gained a certain amount of stability can comprehend that the objects of experience, although the cause of much ill, are not bereft or devoid of Divine presence. An object becomes the source of ill at that moment when the intellect not only objectifies the object, but also objectifies the Divine presence due to which the object exists. Each object, in fact, does not exist in itself. As such the objects of perception are non-real. It follows, then, that the intellect that objectifies the non-real objects too is non-real or apparent. On the disappearance of the object, the intellect too is deprived of the presence of the object. The Divine presence that is immanent in the object of the intellect perishes not with the passing away of the object.

Without the presence of Being even the existence of the non-real object is not possible. Even though the objects are unreal, their substratum, that is, Brahman, continues to be. That which is real remains, and the unreal alone is negated. The delight that is derived from the unity of Being remains constant and continuous through the three periods of time. It is the unchanging Real that is the basis and substratum of the objectivity of objects. The presence of Being exists in equal measure in the expression of each mood. The presence of the Reality exists in same measure in a particle as it exists in a mountain. The Self is the heart of each object and its presence is even and same in every object. The Self is verily different from the body; the body gets born, decays and dies; the self abides, self-same forever.

Friendliness Brings Happiness & Health

Acharya Mahaprajna

The art of being in a state of solitude is called *Prekshadhyana*. Those who have learnt to be in solitude can establish friendliness with the present moment. Now the question arises, "Why is friendliness required?" The answer is, 'search within'. We seek the truth with the help of spirituality and science. Science helps to develop physical and material comforts. But searching for truth through spirituality strengthens friendliness. 'Seek truth within and have friendliness with all'. This is an important message of *Prekshadhyana*. That search for truth which does not culminate in friendliness is not beneficial. Those who nourish the seed of friendliness in life prosper, remain ever delighted, calm and healthy.

Wherever man lives, germs and viruses co-exist in the atmosphere. Naturally, there is sickness. Our bodies have germs and viruses that remain passive for as long as our resistance is good and we remain healthy. Those possessing friendly propensities have strength and resistance, so they always remain healthy. As soon as the emotion of hostility rears its ugly head, the morale gets weakened, and this in turn diminishes the body's resistance. The more vehement the feelings of enmity, the more sickness will afflict man. Medical science has already declared the cause of all the ailments to be germs and viruses. Psychologists add that the cause of ailments is also mental distortion and lack of morale. Those whose morale is weak get easily afflicted and are affected adversely by disease, whereas those with a high morale have a greater capacity to fight the disease and they remain less affected despite having multiple ailments.

The person who has not developed friendliness has an underdeveloped morale. Enmity is so poisonous that it keeps troubling and weakening the morale of whomsoever it infects, creating frustration, hatred and animosity. Hatred, frustration, depression, weakness, jealousy and dejection are ferocious germs that keep eroding one's health and consequently make one sick. Friendliness brings good health. Medicines are only an aid to overcome sickness; from the spiritual point of view you should take shelter in spirituality. Shelter and assistance are entirely separate entities. Though help can be taken from anyone, shelter has to be consciously chosen in spirituality.

The second blessing of friendliness is happiness. Only those who have a burning desire for establishing friendliness can realize happiness. Some people get angry and upset easily, sometimes due to feelings of hatred. Friendliness brings about eternal happiness. A person who has developed friendliness never becomes sorrowful; he remains ever ecstatic. Where there is non-grooming of friendliness, man is instantly tempted to develop hatred and animosity. A person who has developed friendliness can never be provoked by scornful tendencies. Those who have nursed friendliness in their minds will never feel hate or enmity towards any person, howsoever bad or greedy that person may be. His compassionate feelings will be so strong that he would contemplate on how to get that person dissociated from evil and unethical conducts.

When a person named Sangam troubled Mahavira, he was overcome by feelings of compassion and instead of feeling any kind of hatred towards Sangam, Mahavira said, "The world is prospering and getting emancipated by following my preaching and your behaviour is going down."

Friendly emotions help develop a sense of humour. Acharyashree's life is replete with numerous humorous anecdotes. A person from a camp which propounded a philosophy opposed to that of Acharyashree, called on him one day. His intention was not good. He came after the discourse to Acharyashree and said, "My son has disappeared."

Acharyashree sympathized with him and said, "This is really very bad."

The visitor asked, "Sire, should I search for him? If I search for him then will it be a sacred act or a sin?"

Acharyashree said, "You are very strange. When you had your son, you did not ask me whether it would be a sinful or a sacred act. Now when you are searching for him, you are asking me whether it will breed sin or sacredness. The result of your quest will be the same as for having a son."

The visitor got the message and went away silently. There is also the mystery of bioelectricity in our life. Our life is governed by bioelectricity. Hostile feelings reduce the strength of bioelectricity and gradually annihilate it. Those who have a weak bioelectricity of life have neither resistance power, nor happiness and calmness in their life. Actually happiness is nothing but the realization of this bioelectricity of life. Bioelectricity is developed through friendliness with others.

Surrender the Ego, Attain Happiness
Ullhas Pagey

In today's fast-changing world, materialism and stress have become part of our everyday lives. We are constantly looking for answers: How to live a successful and happy life? One way of finding out answers to this question could be to explore the Spiritual Quotient (SQ), relating to our ability to understand and comprehend the spiritual aspects of life, which, contrary to popular belief, are not necessarily connected to religion.

Most of us are familiar with the concept of the Intelligence Quotient (IQ). In the mid '90s, Daniel Goleman started talking about EQ or Emotional Quotient. Danah Zoher and Ian Marshal in their recent work SQ: Connecting with our Spiritual Intelligence observe that 'While computers have IQ and animals can have EQ, it is essentially an SQ that sets human beings apart'. Therefore, for the 'Wheel of Life' to roll smoothly, all the spokes of the wheel — IQ, EQ and SQ — have to be equally developed. The journey from IQ to SQ represents moving from gross to subtle, finite to infinite and from tangible to intangible.

SQ has several dimensions: Compassion, wholeness, self-esteem, gratitude, spirit of surrender and service and the ego. Handling the ego is one of the critical dimensions of enhancing SQ. Ego issues, if not handled with care, can create problems in our personal, social and professional lives. Hence for better relationships, it is very important to understand and handle the ego — both of 'self' and others. Ego stems from our bundle of memories. It gets further reinforced when we repeatedly embrace a particular thought for extended periods of time. We tend to take 'ego positions' based on what happened to us in the past. One of the key aspects of handling the ego is to analyse the way in which our thoughts are organized because our ego is embedded deep into our thought process.

Our thoughts are often organized in a hierarchical order. First of all there is a primary layer of thought which constitutes the core, then there is a second layer, a third layer, and so on. The primary layer represents objectivity of thoughts and maturity whereas the subsequent layers represent subjective interpretations often arising out of perceptions which may be far away from reality.

Shri Ramana Maharishi advised that one should contemplate primarily on the inner core rather than on the secondary and tertiary layer; for once we concentrate on the core thoughts, we will naturally look at the events of life more objectively. Once we are objective and deal with issues with all gentleness, care and with a *sattvik* approach, all our transactions become free from the ego. J Krishnamurthy calls this state of mind as one of 'All Conclusive Awareness'. Staying in this state softens our ego. To handle the ego, one has to therefore promote objectivity, for, with objectivity comes truth. This in turn dilutes the ego. Once our actions originate from the depth of our heart representing the primary layer, the path for ego-free relationships will be paved.

Dealing with the ego becomes easier if we can instil a spirit of 'surrender' in our psyche. The environment around you becomes tranquil and peaceful. Surrendering essentially means crucifixion of our ego, but surrendering becomes a rather difficult and painful process because of our worldly attachments. Krishna in the *Bhagavad Gita* (chapter 18) says, "Fly unto Him for refuge with all your being, O Bharata; by his grace you shall obtain supreme peace and eternal abode."

Krishna advises Arjuna to surrender his ego unto Him. Commenting on this, Swami Chinmayananda says, "The surrender unto the Lord should not be a temporary self deception; it should be done with a total spirit of devotion and with a state of ego-lessness." This was the spirit exhibited by Radha, Prahlada and Hanuman.

The surrendering of ego is often construed as a weakness. On the contrary, the spirit of surrender enhances our quality of goodness which ultimately leads to godliness. But where is God? Vedanta says He resides within us. By surrendering the ego we will be able to perpetually experience Spiritual Actualization, leading to a higher SQ. For, "We are not human beings having spiritual experience, but spiritual beings having human experience."

Young & Dejected? Here's some Cheer

MPK Kutty

Life in society today is becoming increasingly more competitive. This is also reflected in the educational system, where admission to select courses has become almost impossible. At this time of the year, university campuses are normally buzzing with activity. There is excitement and tension in the air. The human quest for power, prestige and wealth is visible in the student-aspirants. The courses that offer the best career opportunities are most sought after. For, a good career means a comfortable life.

Career counsellors on the campuses guide and help young students to make the right choice, taking into account their aptitudes and inclinations. Despite the counselling, most students prefer to opt for only those courses and subjects which hold the promise of a bright future. Their ultimate goal is the 'good life'.

There are others, who, for various reasons, do not seek to study further. Many choose to enter their parents' vocation. This is the trend in families engaged in trading, business, crafts, cultivation and increasingly, in politics. But there is something that is common to both categories of seekers: They have dreams — of a happy future.

However, there's a catch. Not all student-aspirants will get the course of their choice. There are bound to be disappointments since the demand for seats is much more than the availability. But setbacks and lamentations are not the preserve of disappointed students. Some of those who get to realize their ambitions are equally disillusioned. We cry over what we lose — often, we also cry over what we gain.

Two little tear drops were floating down the river of life. One teardrop asked of the other: "Who are you?"

It answered: "I was shed by a girl who loved a man and lost him. And who are you?"

Replied the first teardrop: "Well, I was shed by the girl who got him."

King Solomon, one of the wisest men who ever lived, wrote an account of his experiences and his efforts to find satisfaction and fulfilment in his life. He records: "I undertook great projects; I built houses for myself and planted vineyards. I made gardens and parks and planted all kinds of fruit trees in them...I bought male and female slaves...I also owned more herds and flocks than anyone in Jerusalem before me. I amassed silver and gold for myself...I became greater by far than anyone in Jerusalem before me." Yet, in the end, when he surveyed all his possessions and achievements, he concluded that they represented nothing more than his vanity.

King Solomon then made a deliberate effort to acquire wisdom. However, he soon discovered that although wisdom is desirable, the same fate overtakes the wise man and the fool. He realized that everyone shares a common destiny. He then looked for meaning in the happenings and strivings of men 'under the sun and found that even those few wise men who searched for the meaning of existence — while claiming to have understood — did not comprehend it truly'.

King Solomon also found that the swiftest man did not always win the race; the strongest man did not always win the battle; and wealth did not necessarily accrue to men of wisdom. It was all largely a matter of chance. Success or good fortune does not always go to those who deserve it. So if you are a disappointed student who failed to get admitted to the course of your choice, don't be disheartened. You might not realize your dreams of becoming a doctor or an engineer, but that doesn't mean that you are unfit for any other profession or vocation. Whatever your field of work, take interest in it. Work diligently to the best of your ability. Take pride in your work.

Para Vidya, Path to Eternal Bliss

Shri Ashutoshji Maharaj

Para vidya alone can show us the path to eternal bliss. Mundane knowledge which produces 'intellectualism' cannot confer wisdom on us. Even the most amazing of scientific and technological advances have failed to bring lasting happiness in our lives. The exponential increase in knowledge has, surprisingly, led to more conflicts and destruction. *Para vidya* is transcendental knowledge which leads to wisdom. *Apara vidya* or secular knowledge merely enhances our vision of the outer world. Wisdom is perennial while knowledge is mainly informative and therefore transient. The former is stable, the latter, subject to change.

The Mundaka Upanishad makes a clear distinction between the higher knowledge of the Supreme Brahman and the lower knowledge of the empirical world. According to it, *para vidya* alone is a guide to the realization of Brahman. The treatise also acknowledges the necessity of *apara vidya* as a means to earning a livelihood. The knowers of *apara vidya*, too, strive towards the attainment of the highest reality, though in an imperfect manner.

The Upanishad states that the four Vedas and disciplines like etymology, metrics, astrology, phonetics, rituals and grammar fall in the category of lower knowledge or *apara vidya*. *Para vidya*, however, enjoys an exalted status. In the *Bhagavad Gita*, Lord Krishna tells Arjuna that *para vidya* is the supreme and the most difficult of the sciences. It is all pervading, yet it is beyond the reach of the sense organs; and it is revealed to the seeker by a seer. The Upanishad serves a warning to those who consider ritual as real: 'deluded by sacrifice, austerity, alms-giving, pilgrimage and outer worship, men pass many years in misery'. A similar note of caution is sounded in the Garuda Purana. Sage Katha in Katha Upanishad condemns those who go about flaunting their knowledge of the scriptures, saying: "Abiding in the midst of ignorance, wise in their own esteem, thinking themselves to be learned, (they) go about like blind men led by one who is himself blind." The Upanishad also tells us that the consummate spiritual experience takes place when a seeker sees God through divine eyes. When a perfect sage imparts *para vidya* to the pupil, the bonds of ignorance that fetter him are cut loose, all doubts are dispelled and the fire of this divine knowledge turns all his actions or karmas into ashes. Such is the power of the knowledge of Brahman. On being blessed with *para vidya*, the soul is freed of all attachments, enters the calm stillness of the self and is able to perform tasks without compulsion, for the sake of duty alone rather than out of self-interest or benefit. Its life then becomes a free flow of liberated consciousness, incapable of rest since the living God Himself does not rest. A deep, unmoved repose at the centre and an unbounded, perpetual creativity are the prominent features of such an individual.

The individual then becomes liberated, a *jivan mukta* in the present life. He performs his duties like an actor on stage, freed of any selfish motives. He is not deluded by what he does on stage. He will do his duty impartially, regardless of gain or loss. His concern is with action only, not with the result. He sees action in inaction and inaction in action. This is complete surrender and is the true spirit of renunciation. Just as rivers disappear into the ocean, casting off name and form, the knower of Brahman, freed from name and form, arrives at the supreme reality. Such an individual realizes the universality of the spirit. This is the pinnacle of human perfection, which all scriptures glorify.

Ultimate Pledge for Lasting Happiness

Shri Asaramji Bapu

Sankalpa means taking a pledge to fulfil one's desires. The *Bhagavad Gita* says, "For it is when there is no clinging on his part to the things of senses or to action and when he renounces all *sankalpas* — aims and interests, thoughts, purposes and desires — that he is called a yoga *arurha* or one who has achieved the height of yoga."

There are two types of *sankalpas*: the *mahasankalpa* and the current *sankalpa*. Current *sankalpas* are those everyday mundane desires like eating, drinking and entertainment which keep us happy. Every human being has a *mahasankalpa* or desire: 'I should be always happy. I should never feel sad. I should reach a point from which I cannot fall'. This *mahasankalpa* is hidden deep inside every human mind. All *sadhanas* like meditation, devotion, *satsang*, worship and actions are meant only to fulfil the *mahasankalpa*. Egotism and jealousy are obstacles on the path of attainment of *mahasankalpa*. Thus, if one is freed from all the vices of false-esteem, egotism and jealousy, then *mahasankalpa* will be realized. It is purely on account of their *mahasankalpas* that saints have attained the ultimate goal of self-realization.

Mahasankalpa is therefore the desire to attain permanent happiness through self-knowledge. When the mind is deluded by jealousy and petty sorrows of mundane life, the goals of our current *sankalpas* fade, leaving us with no hope of fulfilling the *mahasankalpa*. Therefore, we have to be cautious that lower desires do not creep into our minds. Chanting helps eradicate futile *sankalpas*. This clears the path for us to attain the *mahasankalpa*. You have to make a conscious effort to overcome the temptation of distractions in your daily life. If you do not make this effort, even your preceptor will not be able to help you.

The scriptures state: 'The foolish person is not enlightened even if the Creator (Brahma) becomes his Guru'. So, it is entirely up to you. This makes it all the more imperative that the current *sankalpas* should be kind, full of wisdom and conducive to the fulfilment of the *mahasankalpa*. And once the *mahasankalpa* is made, the subordinate *sankalpas* move in conformity with it. For example, if "I want to attain God-realization" is the *mahasankalpa*, then, the subsidiary *sankalpas* of mundane life will also be in accordance with the former. The futile *sankalpas* will gradually diminish.

To nurture this *mahasankalpa,* you should take a pledge to attain Brahma Jnana or God-realization in this lifetime itself. The very fulfillment of such a *mahasankalpa* enables one to experience supreme bliss. Then, the illusion of seeking happiness in this world totally vanishes. All those saints who have accomplished self-realization do not have to actively seek happiness; the ocean of bliss and spiritual wisdom is in their *anthakarna* or heart so much so that it is discernible to anyone who is in close proximity.

In fact, this *mahasankalpa* is already present in our minds. As a result of the commendable acts performed by an individual in his past and present lives, he is eventually inspired to realize and fulfil the *mahasankalpa*. This *mahasankalpa* is the Supreme Bliss, which cannot be taken away even by the Lord of Death. Let the critic censure, let the sycophant shower appreciation, but the one whose entire being is enshrined in the *mahasankalpa* and who is blissfully contented, is not distracted by circumstance and contingencies. He is liberated in this life. Call it what you may: *Mahasankalpa*, self-realization or self-knowledge, they are all the same. In fact, happiness is the natural state of your being. To attain permanent happiness, knowing your self should be your *mahasankalpa*.

Thinking it through, you can be Happy

Anil K Rajvanshi

A young boy went to a guru and asked him how he could find God. The guru realized that the boy had spiritual leanings but was far too young to be educated in the abstract knowledge of the Vedas and the Upanishads. He asked the boy who he loved the most. The boy replied, "My calf. I play with him all the time. He is my companion." The guru asked the boy to meditate on the calf. After a few months when the guru went to meet the young disciple, he found him crying. "I am losing my mind," he said. "The calf has become so small that it sits on my palm." The guru advised the disciple to continue meditating on the calf. On his next visit the guru found the disciple crying again. "Now the calf has grown so big that it reaches the sky," he said. The guru asked the boy to continue meditating. Several years passed before they met again. This time, the guru saw that his student had attained happiness — he had reached his destination. After considerable effort he roused the disciple from his samadhi. On coming out of his trance the disciple said, "Sir, you, I, the calf, the sky and God are the same!"

Concentration is the essence of yoga. Focusing your thoughts can produce tremendous happiness. Religions, preachers and gurus have talked about happiness and how to achieve it. Most religions focus on renunciation and the elimination of desire. Some promise happiness in the after-life. However, attaining happiness in this life itself is not impossible. Desire is the engine of progress. It should not be suppressed or removed, but should be sublimated to achieving happiness.

Concentration on a single thought stimulates or 'tickles' the pituitary gland and gives you a sense of well-being. It is also one of the key components of happiness. The inability to do so makes the mind fickle and insecure. Inner peace and security can come only from a calm mind. We need to train ourselves to focus on positive thoughts. Happiness is a state of mind. One may have a lot of wealth and resources and still be miserable. On the other hand, there are people with meagre resources who are happy. One of the main reasons for unhappiness is greed — greed for power, money and other resources.

We are constantly striving to play God. We often come close to achieving this. Our technological innovations could change the very tapestry of nature. Our mortality and our arrogance demand that we accomplish everything in this lifetime. Nature also effects changes, but those changes take place on a geological time scale. Natural systems remain in equilibrium with their surroundings, even while evolving. Changes introduced by humans, however, do not allow for this. That's why we end up disrupting our environment. Greed also causes conflicts among people. Today, most of us suffer from short attention spans. Deep thought requires energy, application and will-power. A short attention span results in low concentration. If we train our children to read and reflect, it will fuel their imagination and motivate them to think originally. A focused person, therefore, has better chances of finding happiness.

We all like to believe that we can change the world. This grandiose desire to change the world creates a lot of unhappiness. Efforts to reform the world must begin small. We need to look at our own attitudes and prejudices before we can think of changing the world. Our thoughts and attitudes reflect our society and culture, and are therefore probably the best place to look. We must remember that all we can really change is ourselves — if we become better human beings then this world will also become a better place to live in.

The Small Boy & the Leaf

Vinay Kamat

He was a small, thin boy with a mole on his face. But what he told our seventh standard class many years ago still bothers me. The moral science teacher had given us homework. We had been asked to write an essay on 'happiness'. We all thought it was easy. But when we started writing it, we realized our limitations. Some of us wrote about the happy moments surrounding birthdays; some spoke of the emotional highs on getting a first in class; others remembered kites and whoops of joy. But the small, thin boy saw nothing in the events that excited us. Nothing at all. He was uninterested. Yes, he was an oddity. He was often lost in his own thoughts though he appeared calm. He asked too many questions, and he answered them himself. He seemed to be searching for a friend and had found one in himself.

His essay on 'happiness' was strange — at least it appeared so at that time. I did not know how to respond to it. Here's what I can recollect from his singular essay: "I do not know what happiness is. I can't define it. Is it a mood? Is it a thought? Is it about innocence? It's difficult. But I did feel happy last Wednesday when I opened my window. The atmosphere was right, there was a light breeze. Just across the window was a cashew tree, it was swaying gently. Something was building within me. And, then, a bright yellow leaf started falling. It circled and circled and fell. I don't know what happened, but I felt nice. It was a positive feeling. I smiled. Yes, you could say, I felt happy. I had never felt like that before." The class of 1977 was certainly dazed. Happiness? Leaf? Small, thin boy with an attitude? If there were any doubts about the eccentricity of the small, thin boy, the essay had put them to rest.

Years have gone by and I still think about the falling leaf and my classmates. Are we taking our lives for granted? Do we see magic in the ordinary? Or are we wasting our time chasing the extraordinary? Are we searching for something that is right in our midst in our very selves? Have we found it? Just imagine what the lonely leaf has set off. It is a symbol of life itself, a friend tells me when I recount the incident of the small, tiny boy. Another interprets it as childlike innocence. The falling leaf, like life, is serendipity, says another friend. "It's everything — and nothing." Indeed, the small, thin boy was explaining cosmic serendipity in his own way. If life is an accident, then let's view it as such. Let living itself be a moment of happiness, however small or large that instant is. At the end of the seventh standard term, I had numerous meetings with the small, thin boy. One day he was franker than ever: "I have often wondered what it's to experience a world without life. I have tried it and found it extremely disturbing. Even as there is a moment of happiness in seeing a leaf, there is sadness in experiencing a world without a leaf. And I am just beginning to understand it.

"Reasoning, intelligence, wisdom, experience, imagination are fine. But they will never help you experience a falling leaf. It has to do with awareness," the boy said. I realize now that he was referring in his own way to consciousness. It's an inner voyage that he had undertaken at a very young age. He had realized then that a leaf is not a leaf; that we must understand ourselves to understand what's beyond us; that awareness delimits our mind; and that awareness, unlike memory, is self-effacing. For there can never be individual awareness. Yet, many years later, I only remember one cosmic individual and a falling leaf.

Give it all Up for the Sake of Bliss
Osho

A religious man, of our old concept, was one who had renounced life and fled the world. How could he sing and dance in a miserable world? He could only cry and weep. He could not play a flute; it was impossible to imagine that he danced. It was for this reason that Krishna could not be understood in the past. He looked so irrelevant, so inconsistent and absurd in the context of our whole past. But in the context of times to come, Krishna will be increasingly relevant and meaningful. And soon, such a religion will come into being that will sing and dance and be happy... The religion of the future will be life-affirming. It will accept and live the joys that life brings and will laugh and dance and celebrate in sheer gratitude...

Rarely could you have come across a person who took to *sanyas* (renounced the world) out of sheer joy. Normally, when a man's wife died and his life became miserable, he turned to *sanyas* as an escape from his misery. If someone lost his wealth, went bankrupt and could not bear it, he took to *sanyas* in sheer despair. An unhappy person, a person ridden with sorrow and pain, escaped into *sanyas*. *Sanyas* stemmed from unhappiness and not from happiness. Normally, no one comes to *sanyas* with a song in his heart. Krishna is an exception; to me he is that rare *sanyasi* whose *sanyas* is born out of joy and bliss. And one who chooses *sanyas* for the joy of it must necessarily be different from the general breed of renunciates, who are filled with misery and frustration. They are only trying to run away from the pain and suffering they experience in the world, wrongly identifying this with the act of *sanyas* whose true meaning is largely misunderstood. True *sanyas* is inspired by joy and happiness and not by pain and misery.

The religion of the future will stem from bliss; the *sanyas* of the future will flow from the joy and ecstasy of life. A man will take *sanyas* not because his family tortures him, but because his family is now too small for his expanding bliss — and so he adopts the whole world as his new family. He will accept *sanyas* not because his love turns sour, but because one person is now too small to contain his overflowing love — and he has to choose the whole earth as the object of his love. And they alone can understand Krishna who understand this kind of *sanyas* that flows from the acceptance of life. The *sanyas* that is born out of unhappiness cannot lead to happiness and bliss. The *sanyas* that arises from pain and suffering can at best lessen your suffering, but it cannot bring you joy and bliss. You can, of course, reduce your suffering by moving away from the situation, but you cannot achieve joy and bliss through it.

Only the Ganges of *sanyas* that is born out of bliss, can reach the ocean of bliss — because then all the efforts of the *sanyasin* will be directed towards enhancing his bliss. Spiritual pursuit in the past was meant to mitigate suffering, it did not aim at bliss. And, of course, a traveller on this path does succeed, but it is a negative kind of success. What he achieves is a kind of indifference to life, which is only unhappiness reduced to its minimum. That is why for many of our old *sanyasins, sanyas* is not alive and happy, dancing and celebrating. To me, Krishna is a *sanyasi* of bliss. And because of the great possibility and potential of the *sanyas* of bliss opening up before us, I have deliberately chosen to discuss Krishna. It is not that Krishna has not been discussed before. But those who discussed him were *sanyasis* of sorrow, and therefore they could not do justice to him. On the contrary, they have been very unjust to him. And it had to be so.

The Ultimate Joy is Inner Growth

Swami Sukhabodhananda

Why do sad people attract sad incidences in life? Why do happy people attract happy situations in life? Why some people are prone to divorce? Why do some people always get a wrong job and wrong boss?

Depending on what state of being we are, we attract situations. We have to focus on heightening our state of being rather than changing situations in life. If our state of being is low, then the external situation, even though sacred, will be pulled down to our level of being. For example, a poor man in a palace will make the palace into a gutter.

Mullah Nazaruddin, while walking in the desert, saw a group of people riding horses. He thought they were robbers and started running. They turned out to be travellers. Seeing the Mullah running, the travellers thought he was in trouble — so they started going towards him. Now the Mullah was convinced they were after him and he ran into a graveyard — the travellers followed him there. The tired Mullah lay down on one of the coffins. Then he realized they were not robbers but travellers. They asked him: "Why are you here?"

"I am here because of you and you are here because of me" answered the Mullah.

'This is the law of karma'. In other words, we attract situations in life. We often find ourselves in such situations aligned to our state of being. If our consciousness is not committed to transformation, then we will not grow wiser from situations, but complain and grumble, expecting the situation to be different.

According to yogic *shastras*, there are different levels of being — seven *chakras* or centres. Some operate from the lowest centre and such people attract similar situations. Nature context is that humans evolve from lower to higher centres. This happens when you learn and grow. If one does not do that then the situation goes on repeating itself until we learn and grow.

How can we change one state of being? There are two types of growth: horizontal and vertical growth. Horizontal growth means more money, name, fame. People's yardstick of growth is more in the horizontal domain. People come and tell me, "I have grown" — which means five years back I earned one million dollars a year and now I earn 10 million dollars a year. This type of growth is not fulfilling. The second type of growth is vertical growth. The yardstick for this is: Five years back how calm was I, and how calm am I now? The growth is measured in its depth and not in its width. The more one grows in love, kindness and compassion, the more one is truly growing. Such a growth is fulfilling. Growth happening in the vertical dimension changes one's state of being.

In ancient India a king sought to resolve a dispute between two of his ministers who wanted to marry the same woman. He told both of them to walk on a rope and whoever did so successfully, would win the hand of the woman. One minister spent a sleepless night worrying how he would be able to walk the tightrope. The other minister was very relaxed — he felt there was no point in getting agitated when death was imminent anyway.

The minister who kept his cool emerged the winner, walking effortlessly on the rope. Asked to share his secret, he only said, "I do not know." To walk on the rope without losing one's balance involves being relaxed, balanced and being in the present. The same qualities are vital for the success of a marriage, too. In order to grow vertically, one has to cultivate the art of relaxation, be balanced, and stay aware in the present. Life is fulfilling only with such a type of growth. Happiness and joy flower forth in this state of consciousness.

Why Small Things can Shatter Happiness

RD Parkar

Who doesn't want to be happy? We all desire happiness. We pursue pleasures systematically through life — it comes as naturally to us as the sunflower turns to the sun. But, pleasure once obtained does not last; so once again, the search begins. Moreover, pleasure is ephemeral; it eludes the seeker at the final moment. One may work very hard and get all that the world considers necessary for a happy life, yet none of these things can make us really happy. Sorrow is a fact of conditioned existence, said Buddha. It is pain and suffering that leads us towards growth. Aeschylus said, "Call no man happy till he is dead," that is, "till he has carried that happiness safely to his grave."

"Accept the woes of birth" advises the Mahayana Buddhist text. One of the implications of this 'acceptance' is resignation and recognition of limitations. Having tried our best to change the situation, we must then learn to resign. Contentment cannot come by looking at those who have more than we have. It comes when we try to look at those who are worse off, who are less fortunate than we are. A Christian saint said, "I cried for boots until I saw a man who had no legs." The more things we require for being happy, the greater our chances for despair and disappointment.

There are several people who do not have even the basic necessities of life and are yet happy. Happiness is a state of mind. This is easier to achieve once we learn to be less self-centred. The more egocentric we are, the more vulnerable we become; even a small thing can shatter our happiness. At the material, intellectual and spiritual levels there is every chance of our being disappointed so long as we are egocentric. It may be something as petty as not being invited to a lunch party; or, if a colleague gets a promotion and we do not, we become unhappy; or if another person is judged kinder and nobler than we are, even then, we tend to become jealous.

Statistically, there is a bell-shaped curve, tapering off, either side, showing that extreme cases are rare. So, extremely good or extremely bad people are rare. We need to cultivate *mudita* or sympathetic joy. If our friend or neighbour is happy, then it should fill our hearts with joy as well. Cultivate detached attachment, since everything is transient. In our happiest and saddest moments, we must remind ourselves: "This too shall pass away."

"In sensation no permanent home can be found, because change is the law of this vibratory existence. It is useless to pause and weep for a scene in a kaleidoscope which has passed," teaches the mystical book, *The Light On The Path*. The ocean of life washes up to us and away again. We are so dependent on outside things and people for our happiness that if any of them are missing we feel thoroughly miserable. Above all, the question is of moulding our self-will. "The way to inward peace is in all things to conform to the pleasure and disposition of the Divine Will." If we want lasting happiness we must be prepared to surrender pleasures of *preyas* or smaller worth for pleasures of *shreyas* or greater worth. True happiness comes about when, even for a few moments, we forget ourselves, making it possible for us to establish contact with our higher nature, the divinity within.

When we are admiring a painting or listening to a piece of music or observing the sunset, we do forget ourselves for those moments. We sometimes experience this bliss when we meditate. We also experience this happiness when we forget ourselves in helping someone or in doing good works without any self-interest. So long as we are searching for happiness, we are bound to be unhappy. But when we cease making happiness our goal, we shall definitely experience it as a kind of by-product.

In Search of Happiness

Anup Taneja

All the misery we experience can be attributed to our failure to understand that true happiness can be attained only when one is able to harmonize with the best thing in him, with the Supreme Divinity, and not with the brute. Happiness constantly eludes one who is dominated by base instincts and in the process suppressing the inner voice of conscience.

"We are all conscious that there is another inside of us; that there accompanies us through life a divine, silent messenger — that higher, better self which speaks from the depths of our nature and which gives its consent, its 'Amen', to every right action and condemns every wrong one," wrote Marden. Men and women in all times have tried to attain happiness by ignoring their conscience that keeps reviewing all their good and bad actions on a constant basis. Therefore, all efforts to buy its approval; to silence its voice in nervous excitement; to drown it in pleasure, with intoxicating substances are bound to go in vain.

The Supreme Being created us along the lines of truth and justice; therefore, in order to gain true happiness it is imperative that we do not violate the laws that constitute the very core of our existence. So long as we continue to indulge in negative practices, for example, to earn money through unlawful means — by accepting bribe or exploiting others — so long as our aspiration is to amass wealth by any possible means, we can never attain true happiness, simply because we have deviated from the path of righteousness. The thought that we can indulge in corrupt practices and then beg the Lord's forgiveness through prayer or by bathing in a holy river; the thought that we can do wrong and be forgiven without atoning for wrong actions, has done more harm than good. He who has a clear conscience, leads a clean life, and is able to obliterate the negative traits of selfishness, jealousy, envy and hatred from the mind.

We tend to make happiness too complicated an affair. Most people are governed by the understanding that happiness can be derived by doing something on a grand scale; from making a big fortune; and from ostentatious display of wealth with the purpose of showing off one's affluence and high status in society. But happiness can be attained from the simplest and most unpretentious things. Pleasure can never be forced; it must come in a natural way, from uncomplicated living. One often hears the statement: "He has the money, but cannot enjoy it." Helping colleagues and friends without expecting anything in return; acts of kindness towards animals; conducting oneself with utmost humility; performance of one's duties with utmost sincerity; protecting the gifts bestowed upon us by bountiful nature; living in a spirit of togetherness with fellow beings — all these are simple things, yet they are what constitute true happiness . And this is what leads us to bliss that lies within reach if only we knew how to access it.

Peace Feeds Happiness

Oswald Pereira

What has peace got to do with happiness? The connection is like that between life and living. For, peace makes life worth living, and paves the way to happiness. Peace and happiness are linked so inextricably that there's no happiness without peace. What comes first: peace or happiness? Could you be at peace if you're not happy? The answer to these questions depends on your idea of happiness ...on whether you get happiness from external factors or from within.

In the *Bhagavad Gita,* Krishna tells Arjuna that no man can know happiness without peace. However, to experience peace, we need to prepare ourselves to receive it; so in a way we are responsible for making peace and happiness happen. For peace and happiness to last, both ought to spring from within, regardless of any turmoil or otherwise that is happening outside. The more you internalize your feelings of peace and happiness, the more the chances are of your reaching blissful heights. Once you are able to source peace and happiness from within, you can transcend external vicissitudes to remain ever-happy and blissful.

Reverend Ernest A Fitzgerald described happiness as a deep sense of inner peace' that comes when you believe that you are 'making a difference for good in the world'. Thomas Jefferson, former US president, said, "It is neither wealth nor splendour, but tranquillity and occupation, that give happiness."

From a Buddhist perspective, too, one can learn that "people inflict pain on others in the selfish pursuit of their happiness or satisfaction. Yet, true happiness comes from a sense of peace and contentment, which in turn must be achieved through the cultivation of altruism, of love and compassion, and elimination of ignorance, selfishness, and greed," in the words of the Dalai Lama. The Buddha said that to "enjoy good health, to bring true happiness to one's family, to bring peace to all, one must first discipline and control one's own mind."

Peace is a recurring prayer in Holy Mass celebrated by Christians. The priest chants, 'Peace be with you' and the congregation replies, 'With you also'. The congregation offers each other 'The Sign of Peace'. The mass ends with a blessing by the priest, 'Go in peace, the mass is ended'. What, then, happens to the non-believer? Is he doomed to turmoil and unhappiness? It would be presumptuous and uncharitable to draw such a conclusion. For, there's peace in the smile of a child; there's peace in the tender touch of one's mother…it's got nothing to do with God or religion, but everything to do with the state of your mind.

Thich Nhat Hanh, the Vietnamese Buddhist monk says that "If in our daily life we can smile, if we can be peaceful and happy, not only we, but everyone will profit from it. This is the most basic kind of peace work." Again, no religious strings attached to peace.

The Vedic idea of peace includes peace in all areas of life — psychological, social and environmental, for instance. The Yajur Veda declares: "Let there be peace in heaven, Let there be peace in the atmosphere, Let there be Peace on Earth… May the waters and medical herbs bring peace, May the trees give peace to all beings, May all the gods be peaceful, May the Vedas spread peace everywhere, May all other objects everywhere give us peace, And may that peace come to us and remain with us for ever." Could there be a more sublime yet secular declaration of peace and happiness?

Scriptural Psychotherapy & Happiness

Hasmukh Adhia

Explaining the last chapter of the Uddhav Gita, which is part of the Srimad Bhagavatam, Swami Visharadanand of Prashanti Kutiram, Bangalore, commented that Indian scriptures give deep insights into psychotherapy: "All unhappiness is born out of psychological condition of mind called *vritis* or modifications." Four such conditions of mind are: *spardha* or competition, *asuya* or jealousy, *tiraskar* or hatred and *ahankar* or ego. These four *vritis* destroy our happiness.

Normally, competition occurs among equals. Jealousy is felt towards those who are thought to be better off than or 'superior' to us, and hatred or contempt is directed towards those we think are 'inferior' to us. Ego is in respect of self. Ego is a feeling that I am someone special. What is wrong in competing; doesn't it lead to progress? Swamiji replied: Competition brings about the attitude of 'doing something only to win' rather than 'excelling to bring out your best potential'. When 'winning' and not 'doing the best possible' is the attitude, it may also lead to use of unfair means as also compromise on quality of work input.

Jealousy is a counterproductive attitude of mind because it prevents a person from seeing good qualities in another person. If someone is wise, a jealous person may think he is a hypocrite, and so not learn from the other's virtues. Hatred and contempt are also negative emotions. Ego makes you do things only to win approval of others. If such approval does not come once in a while then the mind is disturbed and that makes an egoistic person very unhappy. "When all others appreciated my work, why did that fellow not do so?" — This is a typical reaction that prevents one from experiencing peace and happiness.

What, then, is the solution for removing such negative emotions from one's mind? One must feel *samatvam* or oneness to overcome competition, jealousy and hatred. And one must understand the true nature of atma, that is, *sat-chit-ananda*, to overcome the ego. The same *atma* is the indweller of the body of all other persons, whose outward forms may be different. If you understand the real nature of *atma* as the creator of this entire Universe, where is the need for you to feel superior or inferior to others and be egoistic? Also, where is the need to get approval of others in order to be happy? What then is the way out? The Uddhav Gita gives the road map to reach this stage. First of all, you have to keep doing your given duty to the best of your capacity without ulterior motive, ego or 'doership'. This is the path of Karma Yoga. This then will lead to purity of mind which is absolutely essential for enlightenment. After achieving a near-pure mind you could get on to the path of devotion and trust in God, known as Bhakti Yoga. Soon after that you might spontaneously begin to feel the oneness of all beings and supreme love for all, which is the ultimate bliss that one could ever hope to achieve in this world.

The Joyful Child is the Father of Man

Radhika Nagrath

Everyone loves to look at a child. Not many, however, would find an elderly person as interesting or fascinating. We are inadvertently drawn towards a child and its actions. It's also true that every one of us wishes to look younger than our age. Why do we like children? Is it our own desire to look cute, play without inhibitions with no fear of reprimand or something else?

What attracts us first, and what makes an impact on us, is the child's innocence. Even the stoniest of hearts melts before the innocence of a child. Nothing can escape the child's guileless love that equalizes all — whether rich or poor, worthy or unworthy. The child has never faced pangs of jealousy or manipulation and has never tried to impress others but does that what he feels happy doing. To live like a child one must forego the obsession to please others. People will never be pleased even if you stand upside down for them. One out of hundred ways is enough to displease them, leave aside the ninety-nine things done in their favour, suiting their temperament. So why waste time and energy conniving ways to gratify others? From the bottom of one's heart, everybody likes truthfulness as compared to the superficial ways of impressing others. For many of us today, often stressed at work and home, experiencing child-like joy has become a rarity. Everything is a chore; we place ourselves on a perpetually moving treadmill, trudging our way through life. Or we put ourselves in a rocking chair, going forwards and backwards, lulling ourselves into believing all is well, when in actual fact we go nowhere.

When a child goes up and down a staircase, he finds immense joy in the act — which, to us, seems completely unproductive. There is no visible gain in the process but the child is overjoyed whereas we find it useless. We prefer to get enslaved, busying ourselves to preparing endless 'to do' lists, most of the 'to dos' never get done. Why have we forgotten how to be joyful? We don't giggle or break into peals of laughter spontaneously — things we did as a child. An average adult laughs heartily from his belly barely or not even once during a 24-hour period. A child is a born optimist. He experiences joy in every action, because he is oblivious of the result. He is always in the present. He has the fortune to 'realize' the simple joy of being. Adults, on the other hand, tend to either brood over the past or worry about the future, thereby letting slip the precious present. The mother takes care of the child's every need — expressed or otherwise — because the child has surrendered to her unconditionally. As adults, we forget spontaneity. We want things to be done as per our choice, not as per His will. Swami Vivekananda said,

"Let never more delusive dreams veil off thy face from me
My play is done O Mother, break my chains and make me free."

Shed your inhibitions; dance like a child. Be spontaneous; laugh heartily. Look at work and home with new eyes — with the eyes of a child: discover the joy of simple pleasures, learn to live life joyously. Life is not a chore, it is a journey of discovery.